COMPARATIVE
EARLY CHILDHOOD
EDUCATION

COMPARATIVE EARLY CHILDHOOD EDUCATION

By

GEETA RANI LALL, Ph.D.

Educational Diagnostician
Learning Disabilities Consultant
and Remedial Curriculum Specialist
Berrien Springs-Benton Harbor, Michigan

and

BERNARD MOHAN LALL, Ph.D.

Professor of Educational Administration
Andrews University
Berrien Springs, Michigan

CHARLES C THOMAS • PUBLISHER
Springfield • Illinois • U.S.A.

Published and Distributed Throughout the World by

CHARLES C THOMAS • PUBLISHER
2600 South First Street
Springfield, Illinois, 62717, U.S.A.

©*1983, by* CHARLES C THOMAS • PUBLISHER

ISBN 0-398-04777-4

Library of Congress Catalog Card Number: 82-16810

Printed in the United States of America

I-R-1

Library of Congress Cataloging in Publication Data

Main entry under title:

Comparative early childhood education.

    Includes index.
    Contents: Early childhood education in the U.S.S.R. / Bernard
M. Lall and Geeta R. Lall – The education of young children in Israel / Avima D. Lombard and Lynne S. Jasik – Preschool education
in India / Geeta R. Lall and Sushila Poddar – [etc.]
    1. Education, Preschool – Addresses, essays, lectures. 2. Com-
parative education – Addresses, essays, lectures. I. Lall, Geeta Rani,
1934-   . II. Lall, Bernard M., 1929-   .
LB1140.22.C65   1983   372'.21   82-16810
ISBN 0-398-04777-4

DEDICATION

Two lovely people who have had profound influence on our lives are Dr. Keith Goldhammer, Dean, College of Education, Michigan State University and Dr. Mildred Roebeck, Professor of Early Childhood Education, University of Oregon, Eugene, Oregon.

Both are great scholars, outstanding teachers, prolific writers, and above all wonderful friends of students who have had the privilege of working and studying under their supervision and direction.

To Dr. Keith Goldhammer and to Dr. Mildred Roebeck who have devoted their lifetime in the progress of not only Early Childhood Education but all phases of education, we respectfully and fondly dedicate this book.

Geeta Rani Lall
Bernard M. Lall

CONTRIBUTORS

Maurice DuPreez, M.A.
Elementary School Principal
Gary Indiana, USA

Samuel T. Harris, Ed.D.
Assistant Professor of Teacher Education
Andrews University
Berrien Springs, Michigan, USA

Lynne Jasik, Ph.D.
School of Social Work
The Hebrew University of Jerusalem
Jerusalem, Israel

Minette Jee, Ph.D.
Senior Organizer for Infant and Nursery Schools
Lancashire County, U.K.

Geeta Rani Lall, Ph.D.
Educational Diagnostician, Learning Disabilities Consultant,
and Remedial Curriculum Specialist
Berrien Springs-Benton Harbor, Michigan, USA

Bernard Mohan Lall, Ph.D.
Professor of Educational Administration
Andrews University
Berrien Springs, Michigan, USA

Lillian Logan, Ph.D.
Professor of Education
Brandon University
Brandon, Manitoba, Canada

Avima D. Lombard, Ph.D.
School of Education
The Hebrew University of Jerusalem
Jerusalem, Israel

Sushila T. Poddar, M.A.T., M.A.
Associate Professor of Education
Spicer Memorial College
Poona, India

Lisa Heber Østlyngner, Ph.D.
Coordinator, Student Teaching
Oslo, Norway

Masako Shoji, Ph.D.
Professor of Education
Seiwa Women's College
Professor Emeritus
Hiroshima University
Japan

PREFACE

COMPARATIVE *Early Childhood Education* was conceived at the quadrennial session of the World Council of Curriculum and Instruction (WCCI) held at Istanbul, Turkey. It was felt by many attending scholars that a book of this nature would have invaluable impact on international understanding of early childhood education and provide a platform for unity in diversity.

This book has been designed in such a way that it would serve as a textbook for comparative education, comparative early childhood education, and early childhood education classes. It wiii be of help to early childhood educators and people in general who have an interest in early education of children.

In this book, we have included eleven countries in all. In dealing with each country, we have presented information on the basic philosophy, historical development, organization and administration, financing, prevalence, and curriculum of early childhood education. In the last chapter, we have provided a comparison in each of these areas for the eleven countries. Scholars will find this comparison interesting and informative. The intention was to study the various aspects of early childhood education to learn the strengths of each program and not to ponder on the weaknesses.

As we study the philosophy of early childhood education of various countries, we find it interesting to note the basis of their philosophical thoughts. For example, in the USSR, the philosophy is that a child could learn at an early age what he eventually will have to master, whereas, in the USA, early education deals with the child's social, environmental, cognitive, and motor development, which leads to a better understanding of self and environment. Though stated differently, it appears that both countries have similar philosophies: to help children learn in their early years what will help them in their adolescence.

We can find many such similarities and sometimes dissimilarities as we study each country represented in this book. Nonetheless, we are dealing with children—our common denominator—in this book. Children will play, work, and learn in spite of national and cultural barriers. Children, if opportunity is given, will communicate in spite of their language differences, making friends and showing love and understanding for each other.

It is our hope that adults everywhere will find this book useful and rally together to provide early childhood education for the little ones who will grow up to become mature, contributing members of our world society.

Geeta Rani Lall
Bernard Mohan Lall

ACKNOWLEDGMENTS

IN the production of any book, scores of people are involved. It is difficult to remember every person and acknowledge each contribution. However, we wish to publicly thank each international contributor for the materials we received in compiling various chapters for this book. We wish to thank Mr. Ron DuPreez and Mr. Maurice DuPreez for their help in editing and researching untiringly in bringing this work to completion. Cheryl Hunter and Jaycee Palmer, our faithful typists, deserve our heartfelt thanks for their continued support in bringing the manuscript to a publishable form.

To one and all—*Merci beaucoup*, that is, thank you very much.

CONTENTS

COMPARATIVE
EARLY CHILDHOOD
EDUCATION

Chapter 1

EARLY CHILDHOOD EDUCATION IN THE U.S.S.R.

BERNARD M. LALL and GEETA R. LALL

INTRODUCTION

TODAY'S Russian children are the future leaders and citizens of the nation. In this century, children have to absorb the theory of relativity, and they have to cope with automation, television, laser beams, spaceships, and urbanization. Faced with such a society, educators wonder what children should be taught in order to cope with this world of rapidly developing science and technology. The ability to cope helps children gain self-confidence and provides them with the means whereby they can communicate with others, both of which leads to happiness in this world.

The Soviet society spends a lot of time and money on preschoolers for their health, upbringing, and education. The range of facilities provided for preschoolers is divided into two sections: *Yasli* (nursery or creches) for children aged two months to three years old and *Sad* (kindergarten) for children aged three to seven.

Philosophy of Early Childhood Education

Soviet scientific studies have a great influence on the proponents of preschool education. Soviet educator U. Sukhomlinsky, in his book *The Birth of a Citizen*, wrote that, "To rear a person is to foster in him from an early age concern for the present and future of his country. A person's worth is based on his capacity

3

to think, feel, care as a citizen, to acknowledge his duty and responsibility to society. A person in whom these qualities have
been formed will never let society down. On the contrary, he will
perform only good deeds worthy of our ideas, and our society"
(Aksariana, 1975).

Soviet educators say that "90 percent of the child's upbringing
is completed by the time he is five years old." With this in mind,
the problems of preschool education are studied by special institutions such as the USSR Academy of Pedagogical Sciences and by
allied research establishments. Studies in this field, according to
some Russians, show that the foundation of a person's mental
and moral makeup is already established by the age of three or
four (Ibid).

The Soviet philosophy of education emphasizes precocity. The
theory behind this philosophy is that at an early age, the child
could learn what he eventually will have to master. Precocity as-
sures future achievement—the earlier they start, the further they'll
go.

Historical Development of E.C.E.

Shortly after the revolution of October 1917, the new people's
Commisariat (now Ministry) of Education of the RSFRS started
a Directorate of Preschool Education. This Directorate still functions today.

Eighty percent of the women in the USSR work on farms or
in factories. The USSR has thus become a nation of working
mothers, and preschool (*yasli* or *sad*) programs have become an
integral part of society. Nurseries are regarded as preschool establishments; their main function is to offer child care service. This
service is provided for kindergarteners too, along with educational
activities.

Preschool institutions are usually located near the child's
home or near the mother's place of employment. According to
Soviet law, any group—a factory, trade union, collective forum, et
cetera—can start a nursery or kindergarten as long as they are
adequately staffed and have passed government regulations.

By 1955, more than five million children under seven years
of age were in nursery or kindergarten programs.

ORGANIZATION AND ADMINISTRATION OF E.C.E. PROGRAMS

Administration

Programs for preschool education are developed by a joint commission of the Academy of Pedagogical Sciences of the Russian Republic and the Academy of Medical Sciences of the Soviet Union. The Directorate of Preschool Education administers these programs.

Staff

The staff of creches, nurseries, or kindergartens includes a director, teachers qualified in speech training, teacher assistants, a pediatrician, a medical nurse, a music teacher, and a domestic staff including the bursar, cook, and custodial help. The local authority selects the head of each institution and approves or disapproves of the director's selection of staff. The majority of directors are women. Teachers are trained in child psychology and theories of learning and should know how to keep the children involved at all times (*Education in the USSR*, 1958).

Financing of Programs

Preschool facilities receive funding from the state. Despite this funding, tuition fees are charged.

Tuition costs range from thirty to 150 rubles. These fees are charged on the basis of family income, the number of children in a family, the number of hours the child attends school, and the location of the institution. No tuition is charged for children of unmarried mothers, war invalids, parents on disability pensions, and other special cases.

Extent of E.C.E.

Preschool education is provided for children under seven years of age. The programs are broken down into various age groups: junior groups cater to three- and four-year-olds, "preparation for school" groups cater to six- and seven-year-olds, and a combined creche and nursery school caters to children aged two months to seven years.

Besides the ordinary preschools, there are boarding schools where the child remains all week, except for holidays and parents' days off when they go home.

Forest schools are organized for children who are not healthy. These are located out of town, in wooded areas near rivers. The study program is the same as that offered in regular schools and is combined with special treatment, physical culture, and sports.

Schools are provided for exceptional children (blind, deaf, mute, etc.) (*USSR Education,* 1975).

CURRICULUM IN E.C.E. PROGRAMS

The curriculum and programs in preschool education are divided into six groups, which are as follows: (1) Infant group, (2) Second Infant group, (3) First Younger group, (4) Second Younger group, (5) Middle group, and (6) Older group. These groups correspond to the first through sixth years of a child's life.

These programs will now be discussed individually.

The First Infant Group
(First Year of the Child's Life)

The main objectives for this group are the preservation and strengthening of the child's health, proper physical development, and psychological development. It is deemed important to establish a strict daily schedule in relation to the child's age and physical condition.

Positive attitudes need to be developed toward eating, sleeping, working, and dressing. The babies' perceptual skills need to be developed, along with basic motor skills, hand movements, manipulation of objects on a primitive scale, vocal reactions, and aural comprehension.

The infants sleep outdoors in summer and autumn. During spring they sleep on open air patios. The individual who puts them to bed does so while talking to them in soft, soothing tones.

When the babies wake up, they are immediately picked up and fed. Until they are nine to ten months old, babies are fed at home in the morning. Babies who are bottle fed should, at the age of five months, be stretching and grasping for the bottle and should be able to hold it while being fed. By the age of seven to eight months, the infants should be able to hold bread in their hands and feed themselves. The nurse identifies the foods being eaten so as to encourage the baby's speech development. Thus, at the end of the first year the baby should know the names of a few objects.

Babies have to be taught neatness at the outset of life. Therefore, they need to be changed whenever they are wet or dirty. Vocabulary development should also be encouraged in connection with dressing action.

Activities designed to develop the ability to manipulate objects are provided. They include taking rings off a post and putting them on again, opening and closing boxes, and piling blocks. Coordination is developed through activities such as rolling down an incline, and getting the baby to move from one object to another.

Musical Training

Musical training is provided and is regarded as essential in developing within the child an emotional response and encourages the memorization of definite actions connected with it. From the very first month of life the significant adult hums songs while leaning over the cradle and smiling at the baby. She illustrates songs by showing toys to small groups of babies. Such songs include "The Little Bird," "The March," and "From Under the Oak Tree."

The Second Infant Group
(Second Year of the Child's Life)

The objectives for this group are the promotion of health, emotional stability, an active and cheerful disposition, and the development of basic locomotive skills. Other objectives include the development of the senses, development of the ability to comprehend speech, improvement of verbal skills, and the establishment of healthy relationships with peers and affection for parents and adults.

The children have a nap time twice a day. They are also taught to eat bread and soup.

Intensive speech development takes place during this period. By the age of one and a half years, the child should know the names of those around him and also the names of the objects found in the nursery or kindergarten. He should be able to identify the different parts of an animal's anatomy. The child should be able to imitate words and combinations of sounds that are expressed frequently by adults.

Children are encouraged to ask questions and to converse with the teacher. Simplified forms of words in the child's vocabulary are replaced by correct forms and complete sentences.

Play

Games that are played incorporate "subject" toys, education toys, and construction materials. These are arranged inside and outside the building.

By the time the child is one and a half years old, he should be able to play with "subject" toys in a meaningful way. He can gradually substitute real things for "subject" toys, e.g. soap instead of a block, a thermometer instead of a stick.

Musical Training

For children one and a half to two years old, the teacher sings songs accompanied by appropriate body movements; the children may hop on one foot or march with raised and outstretched arms. Musical activities for children between the ages of one and one and a half years are conducted two or three times a week, while children one and a half to two years old have music twice a week.

The First Younger Group
(The Third Year of the Child's Life)

The objectives of this group are educationally oriented; the physical and emotional needs are taken care of on a continuing basis. The educational objectives are to broaden the child's orientation to his surroundings, to improve coordination, to develop group facilitation, simple habits, and independence, and to instill in the children an interest in and a love for music, poetry, singing, and stories.

A single schedule is set up for children at this age level. However, activities are carried out in subgroups. At this stage, the child is expected to be able to wash his hands before meals, eat neatly, and use his right hand predominantly. By the end of the third year, he is encouraged to hold a spoon correctly and put it away after he has cleaned it. He has to remain at the table until he has finished his meal and is taught not to interfere with other children.

Everyday events are used as a springboard for language development. The child should be able to say "hello" and "goodbye" and express his needs in words, speaking in a calm controlled manner, without yelling.

Play

Many games are played without having a definite theme or subject. Children play with balls and spin tops. They not only handle toys but also sort them according to size, color, shape, and texture. They run, jump, skip, roll, crawl, et cetera.

The teacher provides direction to children's play. She also provides materials and tells them how to use them, for example, load dolls onto wagons, build a house with blocks, throw balls into a bucket, et cetera. Games such as hide-and-seek and tag are also played, the teacher demonstrating how it should be played.

During this year, independent activities increase in number with games such as dancing in pairs, turning around and running in opposite directions, and other organized games. The child is expected to have mastered the ability to draw with a pencil and to use clay constructively.

In using the pencil, the child should be able to draw straight, curved, and zigzag lines. In using clay, the teacher will model something, ask the kids to identify what she has made and then get the kids to copy what she has made using their own clay.

Speech Development and Orientation to the Environment

Activities in these areas include systematic observation (watching snow removal crews), excursions (to a park or woods), educational games, and working with pictures. The children will discuss what they saw, will make up and tell fairy tales, read stories, poems, and anecdotes and will be involved in activities using modeling and building materials.

Musical Training

The child should recognize and pay attention to familiar songs and melodies played on the piano or some other instrument. In musical "subject" games, the children role-play and perform various actions according to the mood and character of the music, e.g. horses galloping, birds sleeping, waking, and flying away. In exercises and dances, the children progress from slow movements to fast movements, paying close attention to dynamic and pitch levels in the various parts of the music. They walk or run in pairs while holding hands and dance around in a circle with a student in the middle of the circle.

The Second Younger Group
(Fourth Year of the Child's Life)

The objectives for this group include the continuation of the physical development and care of the child and the ability to play together. They are also taught to respect their elders, follow orders, speak the truth, and develop a knowledge of and proper attitude toward their environment. They also need to develop an interest in music, poetry, and pictures and should know how to create objects with their hands (clay modeling).

Delivery System

A strict schedule is followed so that the child knows what to expect each day.

An exercise period is planned for four or five times weekly, starting with the second quarter of school. These periods last for four to five minutes. The exercises include two or three drills that closely resemble games and are imitative in nature.

At this age, the child can wash his hands and face, roll up his sleeves, dry himself, and sit down at the table for a meal. He can eat unhurriedly, chewing the food thoroughly while holding a spoon correctly. He also uses napkins to wipe his mouth.

The teacher must motivate the children to work and to accomplish something on their own. The children help maintain order in the common room and on the playground and help set the table for meals. The teacher provides the materials and the motivation for activities.

Speech Development and Orientation Towards the Environment

The children are taught to memorize the names of those around them. They are taught to interpret the actions of others, and they are taught to express their desires and requests orally, politely saying "hello," "goodbye," and "thank you" to adults and children. They are taught to distinguish things and name them correctly, e.g. near, far, left, right. Their time concept is also developed, e.g. morning, afternoon, yesterday, today. They learn to observe weather conditions (cold, hot) and can distinguish between animate and inanimate objects. They can recognize the properties that make up sand, water, and snow, and they become familiar with plants, vegetables, and trees by planting their own gardens.

The nature corner and outdoor walks are used to acquaint the child with birds, insects, and domestic animals. They learn about their surroundings, feeding habits, and movements, et cetera.

Children should know the duties of those around them—the teacher works and plays with them, the nurse brings food and washes the dishes, the doctor cures children, et cetera.

Play

Play is organized for the purpose of keeping the child busy, developing sociability and cooperation in a friendly and organized manner, and adding breadth and depth to the child's ideas about his environment. Play also serves the purpose of inspiring curiosity and observations and develops speech, thought, and imagination. "The teacher himself organizes games with several children or a single child, gives out new toys, and helps determine what to play and how to distribute roles. The teacher might show the children a puppet show or wind up toys or tell them a fairy tale" (Bronfenbrenner, 1969).

Different types of games are introduced to this group. Active ones such as ball games develop flexibility and coordination of hands. Education games teach the children colors, sizes, and shapes. Musical education games teach auditory perception, while building games enrich the child's sensory experiences.

Activities

During this year of life, the child's speech and comprehension of adult's speech improves and develops rapidly. In conjunction with this, explanations, instructions, and stories also improve in difficulty. The teacher should alternate difficult activities with easier ones so that the child's attention span is maintained over a longer period of time.

Artistic Literature

The teacher stimulates an interest in books in children. They are encouraged to tell jokes, make up stories, and recite poems.

Computation

Children learn the concept of quantity. They can distinguish "one" from "many." They use containers to compare the quantities that they hold. They are also taught the rudiments of counting by reproducing the teacher's "tap" on the table.

Musical Training

Musical training seeks to evoke in the child a joyous mood. It also develops in children the ability to listen to and appreciate music, recognize familiar tunes, and develop good singing voices and posture while singing; they also learn to dance to the music.

Holidays and birthdays are celebrated by singing songs, reading poems, and performing dances. Children bring gifts and party goods for the child who has a birthday.

The Middle Group
(Fifth Year of the Child's Life)

The main objectives for this group include the continuation of the preservation and strengthening of the children's health and physical development. They need to be trained to tell stories and pronounce words and sounds correctly, and they should develop an interest in nature, books, and people. The qualities of truthfulness and respect for elders also need to be taught.

Delivery System

The daily schedule is followed strictly. Each activity takes place at the appointed time. The children shouldn't have to wait for their meals or their outdoor play periods.

Conditioning

All the activities take place in rooms where the vents are open on cold days and the windows are open on warm days. Cool air, even in winter, serves as a basic means of conditioning the children. The children are dressed very lightly when they are indoors.

Exercises are done every morning for five to six minutes. Three or four drills are used for the various groups of muscles with each drill repeated four to six times.

Cleanliness and Courtesy

Independence is stressed in this area. The child should be able to dress, undress, tie shoelaces, undo buttons, and help peers do the same. Health habits also need to be learned. Children are trained to do various kinds of work. At the beginning of the year, dining room duties are assigned. In the fall and winter, the children help pick up leaves and clear the walkways of snow.

Speech Development and Orientation to the Environment

The children learn to name various furnishings and personal articles. They also learn the qualities and properties of various objects, i.e. size, shape, color, content, etc. They learn to understand and apply temporal and spatial concepts and recognize the different methods of transportation (bus, train). By gathering information about their surroundings, children are learning their native language, its vocabulary, and grammatical structure.

By the end of the year, the child should be able to pronounce all the sounds in the Russian language correctly. They are also able to tell stories in their mother tongue (which may not be Russian).

The children's play is organized in such a way that activities immediately preceding play periods prepare the child's physical and mental faculties for the forthcoming activity. By informing the children when the play period is over, the teacher helps them make the transition from play to activity.

For the various games to be successful, materials that are appropriate and sufficient need to be provided. These would include toy animals, dolls, toy vehicles, furniture, dishes, and clothes.

Group activities would include imaginary exercises such as taking a cruise on a ship, driving a car, or going on a camping trip.

Activities

Directed, structured activities are conducted for periods of fifteen to twenty minutes. In these activities, the children are taught to concentrate and listen to the teacher's instruction and act accordingly.

Familiarization with Nature

The children learn about domestic and wild animals from books, pictures, and from visits to zoos. They learn to identify the animals, what their habits are, and how they are useful to people. They also learn about birds, fish, frogs, and insects.

The children are taught to identify the various parts of a tree, e.g. branches, leaves, needles. They have the opportunity to observe the falling leaves in the autumn and thus learn something about the cycle of a plant organism; they learn the names of plants and flowers in the school garden and also those in nearby fields, and they plant their own gardens and can observe the transformation of a small seed into a beautiful plant.

Artistic Literature

Artistic literature increases the child's interest capacity and adds a new dimension to his personality. They learn to read and recite with expression and feeling. This adds a new dimension to their verbal capabilities.

Computation

The child is taught to count up to five. He learns to compare objects according to size, shape, texture, weight, etc.

Art

The activities in this area are designed to stimulate in the child a lasting interest in the various types of graphic art. These activities also develop aesthetic appreciation and a sense of color, rhythm, and form. One activity period per week is devoted to drawing and modeling with clay. Specific activities are scheduled on a progressive scale for each quarter.

Musical Training

Musical training develops an appreciation for music and helps the children sing together, thus exercising their vocal chords. The child learns to perform individually and in conjunction with others. He learns to coordinate movement in time to the music. The child is trained to carry a tune, which develops his aural music capabilities.

The child is taught to sing in a natural voice, not straining his delicate vocal chords by yelling. He learns to hold long notes while singing. Specific music activities are planned for each quarter.

The Older Group
(Sixth Year of the Child's Life)

The objectives for children in this group are to broaden their concept of their environment and nature and to cultivate their powers of curiosity, observation, and thought. Other important objectives include training in their natural language, the development of an enjoyment for work, respect for elders, and love for the Soviet homeland.

Delivery System

Organization and structure play an important role in the education of these children. As self-sufficiency increases, the time alloted for activities such as eating, sleeping, and preparing for play is decreased. This depends on the teacher's organizational skills. Self-reliance is a natural progression in the development of the child.

Cleanliness and Courtesy

At this age, children should be polite. They are taught personal hygiene, and they learn to take care of their clothes. They know that they need to cover their mouths and turn away whenever they sneeze or cough.

Work

Positive attitudes toward work are established. The children can distinguish between work and play and begin to develop good work habits and skills.

The teacher gets them to perform tasks voluntarily and efficiently. Safety rules are carefully observed. They are taught to take care of the tools and know that they have to be put away when not in use. The teacher assists the children in developing collective patterns.

Independent Activities

The teacher sets up a systematic program that provides practice for the children in various types of work activities and work habits. At this age level, the children are expected to have the ability to set the table for breakfast and dinner and clean the table after meals without outside help. This should be done properly, even though there may be distractions in the room.

The nature corner provides the children with opportunities for plant care. They are required to water the plants and dust and wipe the leaves. Birds and animals are fed under adult supervision. Bird baths and cages are cleaned, and the water in the fish tanks is changed.

The children learn to make simple objects out of cardboard, plywood, and pine cones. The teacher first demonstrates the techniques to the children who work in small groups once a week.

Patriotism

The teacher tries to instill in the children a love for their country. The children are taught songs and poems commemorating important holidays, and they are shown portraits of Lenin and told how much he has done for their people.

Artistic Literature

The children are taught to convey the main thoughts of a book or a story. They memorize and recite or write out poems in their native tongue. They are taught to use expression and feeling when reciting or reading literature. They can describe pictures and paintings and can make up stories about what they see. They develop the ability to answer questions regarding what they read, and they learn to understand the highly expressive language of traditional fairy tales, poems, and stories.

Computation

The children are taught to count from one through ten. They can perceive quantities and are taught to make right and left turns. They learn to sort objects according to shapes, colors, weight, and size.

Physical Education

The children engage in various exercise drills. They also learn to adopt the proper initial positions for these exercises. They are taught to balance while running and walking. They learn spatial orientation and follow the teacher's commands regarding direction and speed.

Musical Training

Musical training stresses appreciation for music and singing. The children are taught to carry a tune and learn the elements of pitch, rhythm, and tempo. Singing also develops correct posture.

FACILITIES USED IN E.C.E. PROGRAMS

Preschool centers usually consist of two-story buildings for nurseries and three-story buildings for kindergartens. They are situated in the middle of microdistricts, surrounded by other buildings. Trees and shrubs cover the grounds, which are used as play areas in good weather. In bad weather, the children play in sheltered areas.

The playground is equipped with dollhouses, spaceships, toadstools, and other materials. These are all constructed with the children's size in mind (Aksarina, 1975).

SUMMARY

Soviet educators believe that a person's mental and moral makeup is established by the age of three or four. Based on this belief, great emphasis is placed on preschool education. Their philosophy of education also emphasizes precocity, and preschools are operated towards this end.

Approximately 80 percent of the women in the Soviet Union work outside the home; one can see the need for careful supervision of their children. Preschools have thus become an integral part of society.

Preschool programs are divided into six groups, corresponding to the first through sixth year of life. These programs are operated on a quarter system. Among the objectives of these programs are the physical and psychological development of the child, social skills, language development, and aesthetic appreciation.

The children are encouraged to perform to their fullest potential. Collectivism and patriotism are also taught.

REFERENCES

Aksarina, Smirnova N.: *Social Education of Preschool Children in the Soviet Union*. Moscow, Novosti Press Agency Publishing House, 1975.

Bronfenbrenner, Urie.: *Two Worlds of Childhood*. New York, Simon and Schuster, 1917.

Chauncey, Henry, ed.: *Soviet Preschool Education, Vol I*. New York, Holt, Rinehart & Winston, Inc., 1969.

————. *Soviet Preschool Education, Vol. II*. New York, Holt, Rinehart & Winston, Inc., 1969.

Children in the USSR. Moscow, Novosti Press Agency Publishing House, 1973.

Education in the USSR. Washington, United States Government Printing Office, 1958.

Fundamentals of Legislation of the USSR and the Union Republics on Public Education. Moscow, Novosti Press Agency Publishing House, 1975.

The Soviet System of Public Education. Moscow, Novosti Press Agency Publishing House, 1973.

USSR Education. Moscow, Novosti Press Agency Publishing House, 1975.

Chapter 2

THE EDUCATION OF YOUNG CHILDREN IN ISRAEL

AVIMA D. LOMBARD and LYNNE S. JASIK

ISRAEL is a young, new country with an ancient history. It has a growing, developing society with ongoing, evolving, changing educational programs. Israel is both an Eastern and a Western society, as it is composed of settlers from all corners of the Earth. Its system of education reflects a diversity of inputs and backgrounds, with religious and nonreligious groups, Arab and Hebrew sectors, and a multitude of spoken languages.

In spite of the many contrasting aspects of the land of Israel, a salient unifying feature of the country is its full commitment to early childhood education. Ninety-seven percent of its four-year-olds, 88 percent of its three-year-olds, and 56 percent of its two-year-olds are in preschool group settings (Egozi & Bielecky, 1980). In the 1976/77 school year, 8.33 percent of all government education expenditures went to preschools. Free, compulsory kindergarten education is provided for five-year-olds, and almost 100 percent of all children in this age group attend kindergarten (Israel Central Bureau of Statistics, 1980). Tuition for children under five is government subsidized on a sliding scale according to family need.

Early education in Israel is generally divided into three broad frameworks: Day Care, Government Preschools, and Kibbutz Preschools. Within each of these frameworks, there is a further subdivision into either religious parochial or nonreligious programs, depending upon the specific orientation of the community or funding agency. Funding in all situations is divided between the central government and the operating organizations, be they private organizations, the municipalities, or the kibbutzim. For each framework (day care, government preschools, and kibbutz preschools), there is a separate program for teacher training and ongoing supervision.

An inherent part of the ancient Jewish cultural tradition is a mandate to the community to provide education for all children from the age of five. It was the custom to expose children to the "atmosphere" of learning from the age of three, with these "preschoolers" attending school but not expected to participate unless they wanted to. It is not surprising, therefore, that some aspect of community responsibility for early education has always been present in modern Israel.

GOVERNMENT PRESCHOOLS

There were over 5,000 government funded preschool classes accommodating 264,000 children between the ages of three and six in 1979-80 (Israel Central Bureau of Statistics, 1980). Registration is on a neighborhood basis. Parents may choose either a general or a religious school. Class composition generally reflects the ethnic representation of the local community. While an attempt is made to group the children by age, frequently classes have children whose ages span a two year range (3-5, 4-6).

Registration and Supervision

A special department within the Ministry of Education and Culture is responsible for government-funded preschool classes. At its head is a national supervisor who serves as both director of the department and liaison between the department and other sections of the Ministry. Although the maintenance (and construction) of preschools is the responsibility of local authorities, the Ministry prescribes the curricula and programs for all schools, provides for the certification, placement, and pay of all preschool teachers, and maintains a system of supervision over all preschool classes. The Ministry of Education and Culture is also responsible for curricula and facilities for the education of teachers for preschool programs.

There are 130 supervisors and eighty field instructors working in the six regions into which the country has been divided by the Ministry of Education for administrative purposes. The supervisors are generally kindergarten teachers with at least ten years of experience and additional training. Field instructors are master teachers with several years of experience in guiding student teachers. The supervisors carry a greater administrative load, while the field instructors' work is primarily directed toward on-site instruction of kindergarten and nursery teachers. The supervisors are responsible for 120 to 130 kindergartens. Field instructors, on the other hand, deal with no more than thirty-six kindergartens, each of which is selected as in need of intensive and ongoing guidance.

Because this large number makes on-site supervision difficult, a great deal of supervisory contact with teachers is maintained through group meetings and regional training sessions on curriculum topics. Supervisors are instrumental in the development of curricular guidelines and serve on a variety of committees within the Ministry dealing with problems of instruction. The national supervisor is responsible for the work and ongoing training of the field supervisors and makes regular field visits with each supervisor. She holds monthly meetings for all supervisors and field instructors and provides opportunities for improvement of each supervisor's knowledge and skills wherever possible.

Kindergarten Teachers

One certified teacher works with a class of thirty to thirty-five chldren. Preschool teachers are prepared in teacher training colleges or seminaries where they undergo two to three years of training after at least three years of high school. There has been an unfortunate tendency for the better educated students in teacher training institutes to move on to high school teaching and for the less successful ones to specialize as preschool teachers. However, the Ministry of Education and Culture maintains an ongoing program of in-service training and encourages advanced studies for those who qualify. In the Jewish preschools, all teachers are women, but in the Arab schools, where men still retain the traditional role of educator and 54 percent of Arab elementary school teachers are male, a small number continued this tradition in the kindergarten until very recently (*Statistical Abstracts*, 1980-81).

Support Staff

Teachers are assisted by a nonprofessional aide. Aides are women who are chosen for their willingness to work with young children but who generally have had limited education. In the standard division of tasks, the aide assumes responsibility for the housekeeping aspects of the preschool activities (preparation of snacks, clean-up after eating) and assists the teacher in routines such as dressing the children for outdoors, wash-up, etc. She is free to work directly with the children only between these tasks and generally for no more than half an hour at a time.

Specialists also work with the preschools. There are regular visits by a rhythmics teacher and a public health nurse. Medical, dental, psychological, and other therapeutic services are available for the children who need them.

Facilities

Preschool classrooms contain thirty to thirty-five children and are usually housed in specially constructed preschool buildings, located either near an elementary school or in a central spot in local neighborhoods and villages. In the Arab sector, on the other hand, kindergartens are usually housed in the same building as the primary schools. Preschool buildings are commonly designed to include two classes in one building, with shared toilets, washroom, kitchen, and an administration reception area located near the front entry. In structures that were not designed as preschools, however, a single class as well as three or four classes to a building can be found.

Equipment

Adequate child-size furniture and major equipment are basic in all preschools. Classrooms are well equipped with a variety of materials. In addition, teachers are provided with a budget for the purchase of educational supplies and materials so that the physical aspects of preschool classrooms reflect the individual personality and interests of the particular teacher. Some of the more commonly found facilities and materials are bulletin boards, child-size straight chairs, chalkboards, phonograph and music-listening materials, running water, tables for working, balls, unit-table blocks, floor blocks, library storybooks, carriages and buggies, clay, plastilene, collage materials, cooking materials (both toy and adult) and housekeeping toys, crayons, dolls and accessories, easels and accompanying supplies, fingerpaints, hospital corner toys, math materials, wood and cardboard inlay puzzles, rhythm instruments, science materials, table toys, and both multi-use creative and highly defined play trucks, cars, trains, and boats.

Outdoor facilities and equipment are less well-stocked in Israeli public preschools. Although most outdoor play areas have adequate space and are properly fenced and cleared for safety purposes, the equipment is relatively sparse. Typically, there are a few pieces of climbing apparatus, a sandbox, three to four swings, no tricycles, and a few pieces of construction equipment. A corner of the play area is sometimes set aside for gardening by the children.

Curriculum

The curriculum in Israeli preschools is predominantly content-centered. Traditionally, the preschool setting was the framework within which children of immigrant parents were first exposed to the evolving rebirth of a common Hebrew culture. Whereas their parents spoke a multitude of languages, almost all first graders were relatively skilled in Hebrew following several years of preschool education. Although there is no longer such a pressing need for a content-centered program with emphasis on holidays, songs, traditions, and the like, the preschool curriculum appears to have solidified into a code that cannot easily be broken. The Ministry of Education and Culture, for instance, has carefully defined and fostered the introduction of a curriculum that would provide intensive enrichment in cognitive and visual-motor skills. Excellent programs and materials are now available for use in such a curriculum, but preschool teachers are slow to avail themselves of them.

Israeli education patterns in general tend to be oriented to the group rather than to individuals. While the child's identity as an individual is in no way clouded, there is as much emphasis placed on the child as a member of the group as on his development as an individual. The children work and play in groups that are most often self-selected or minimally structured by the teacher. The teacher directs classroom activities in a manner that is definitely controlling, while at the same time allows a great deal of freedom and decision making by the children. The schedule for a day, for instance, is determined and controlled by the teacher, but during a given activity period a child may select both the task and the group with which he will be involved.

Conflicts between children and other disciplinary problems are treated gently. Teachers generally try to control the child's behavior verbally through both reinforcement and reasoning. There is relatively little punishment in any form, and physical punishment is a rarity.

Preschool teachers enjoy a large measure of freedom in planning and running their programs. Although standards must be met, there are few restrictions placed on a teacher's pursuing most forms of intellectual, artistic, or social development programs. On the contrary, the Ministry of Education encourages innovation and movement away from the tradition-bound curriculum. It would like to see more emphasis on cognitive, visual-motor, and social skills, with most of the teaching done in small groups.

This move toward an emphasis on intellectual skills represents a relatively new phase in the curriculum for preschools. Early public kindergarten education in Israel was fashioned after the traditions of Froebel and Pestalozzi, but with each new wave of immigration, the nature of preschool education changed slightly. The theories of Montessori and Dewey, for instance, were incorporated into the preschool programs in successive periods prior to the establishment of the State. In the kibbutzim, on the other hand, early preschool education was psychoanalytically oriented, emphasizing the emotional and social growth of the young child through play, and this orientation persists to the present.

The mass immigration that followed the establishment of the State in 1948 brought serious problems for educators. For the first time, the country had to cope with large numbers of children who not only lacked the language of the schools but were intellectually unprepared for the demands of school. Israel suddenly faced a problematic situation whereby more than 50 per cent of the children entering school were educationally disadvantaged. As in earlier periods, the preschools were seen as a first step in alleviating the problem. New curricula and techniques of instruction were not readily available, however, and in the years that followed, teachers, researchers, and administrators worked steadily to identify the deficits with which the children entered the school situation and to develop appropriate programs.

The Intensive Instruction Program, which is currently recommended in preschools with disadvantaged children, is one response to the demand for a new approach to these children. The fundamental change for which the program calls is that the teacher assess the children's progress in terms of processes as well as products. Emphasis is placed on language and perceptual skills, fundamental concepts in mathematics and science, persistence in dealing with problematic didactic materials, and an increased awareness of the immediate environment. Teachers are asked to recognize the deficits with which the children come to the preschool class so as to seek ways of overcoming them. Parent involvement, stronger emotional ties between teacher and child, increased reinforcement for classroom activity, and concentrated focus on the child's performance and talking are suggested means for meeting the problem of the disadvantaged child's negative self-image and his comparative lack of readiness for school. In her description of the fundamentals of the Intensive Instruction Program, Mrs. Naftali (1968) suggests that this preschool program is built around two axes. The one is the child's free play and creativity; the other is the supportive, directing teacher who looks for opportunities to move the child along a steady course of development. The balance struck between these two is the product of the interaction between each teacher and her class.

Daily Schedule

The daily schedule follows a general pattern combining free play, quiet table activities, and group discussions. A typical day might be scheduled as follows (Ministry of Education and Culture, 1966):

8:00--8:30 Children arrive and join in outdoor play, free table activities, or group exercising—the activity varies from

	class to class.
8:30–9:30	Free indoor activities; tables are set up for creative work, children are free to choose a play corner, painting, or any indoor activity.
9:30–10:15	Formal group discussion. The whole class participates in a discussion led by the teacher. This frequently includes demonstrations, teaching songs, preparing festival programs.
10:15–10:45	Wash up and snack time.
10:45–11:45	Free outdoor play; one adult is outdoors with the class, but no games are organized and equipment is used with minimal supervision. Small groups of children may work with the teacher indoors in twenty-minute periods on special materials.
11:45–12:30	Directed indoor activities; the tables are set up with didactic materials, and children are distributed among the activities by the teacher. The teacher moves from table to table, guiding children in small groups.
12:30–1:00	Story time; this can be any quiet activity in which the whole class participates.

This schedule is different in preschools that have religious education as part of their curricular objectives. Approximately 36 percent of preschool classes fit into this category, and their schedules would include a short prayer period at the beginning of the day, blessings before and after eating, and a greater concentration on religious subjects throughout the curriculum.

Parents of preschool children are not actively involved in the daily program of preschools but are asked to help in preparation for holiday celebrations, in the decoration and maintenance of the preschool facility, and as extra hands on field trips. Preschool teachers report to the parents on the children's progress two or three times yearly. The report is in the form of a short scheduled conference at school during the evening hours. Many preschool teachers also make home visits at least once yearly.

Record keeping is uncommon. Most teachers keep very meager records on the children. The Ministry of Education requirements in this area are minimal and additional records are usually kept only in response to specific demands of the kindergarten supervisor.

DAY CARE

A variety of volunteer agencies maintain preschool day care centers attended by over 27,000 children ages six months to four years, representing over 38 percent of the children in this age group (Ministry of Education and Culture, 1979). Some two dozen religious, political, and civic organizations provide such day care, but the bulk of the centers are maintained by two large women's organizations. These programs provide children of welfare recipients and working mothers with care from about six months to school age. The content of the daily program varies from center to center, but in general, it is of a custodial nature until about age four.

In recent years, there has been a growing awareness of the need to upgrade the level of educational input in the day care centers. To this end, a system of educational supervision and in-service training has been developed with the encouragement and support of the Ministry of Education and Culture and the Ministry of Social Welfare (including the Ministry of Labor).

There is general public demand for increasing day care facilities, and this is reflected in a growing number of centers and programs for staff training.

As a result of this increase in services for the very young, there has been an upsurge in the provision of commercial materials and equipment for the education of young children, providing sorely needed resources that were previously very limited.

KIBBUTZ PRESCHOOLS

A kibbutz is a "voluntary collective community, mainly agricultural, in which there is no private wealth, and which is responsible for all the needs of the members and their families" (*Encyclopaedia Judaica*, 1971). Communal care of the children is a singular characteristic of the kibbutz. Children live in groups in children's homes and spend leisure hours only with their parents.

For children raised in a kibbutz preschool, education is somewhat different. At about six weeks of age, an infant is placed in the kibbutz baby home. Until the age of one and a half, babies live together in very small groups in the baby home. Some time before the age of two, depending upon the maturity of the child, number of children and availability of staff, together with his agemates, the child is moved to a toddlers' home, where he remains until of nursery school age. When he is considered ready, he progresses to the preschool groups, where he is housed and taught along with children aged three and a half to seven in an ungraded sequence through first grade. This pattern varies from kibbutz to kibbutz, but common to them all is the progression of a child in an age grouping, through the early steps of his education, on the basis of "readiness" rather than as a result of class structuring and sequencing.

The kibbutzim maintain close contact with a central psychological guidance center and are generally prepared to experiment with and try new techniques and materials to produce what they consider to be better educational results.

Recent developments in the kibbutzim suggest that the practice of communal child rearing may be altered in the years to come. The younger generation of kibbutz Sabras, those born and bred in Israel, is moving toward greater participation of the family in the raising of children. Many kibbutzim now have children sleeping in their parents' quarters, and the function of children's houses will probably change if this trend persists.

ADDITIONAL SERVICES AND PROGRAMS FOR YOUNG CHILDREN

The special focus on early childhood in Israel is reflected in additional government programs for young children. The Ministry of Health maintains a highly developed program for pre- and postnatal care of infants. Over 90 percent of Israeli mothers are involved in this program, since the care given is free of charge and the "Mother and Child Health Centers" have earned the reputation for excellence over the years. Emphasis in this program is on health, nutrition, and physical care with special focus on early identification of developmental problems. A mother and child are seen regularly until the child is three or four years old. Health records are kept on the children and the public health nurse with whom the mother has regular contact frequently acts as general consultant and child care guide.

The Ministry of Education and Culture, sensitive to the special needs of children and the country's diverse population groups, supplements its regular preschool programs through a variety of projects.

Programs designed to improve the educational well-being of the children focus on (1) teachers, through specialized intensive training programs and via in-service education preservice programs, (2) parents, with the objective of involving them more actively in the education of their preschool children (Lombard, 1981; Nir, 1973), (3) children with special needs, by provision of additional teachers trained in special education to guide the integration of handicapped children into the regular kindergarten classroom setting, and (4) provision of special language enrichment programs offered by a specialist within the regular classroom for children with language difficulties.

A network of Pedagogical Centers operates throughout the country in towns and cities. These centers offer teachers an opportunity to view and borrow written audio-visual materials, consult with an early childhood advisor who is generally a master kindergarten teacher, and meet with other teachers in get-togethers and supervisory instruction sessions.

The Center for Educational Television prepares and presents television programs geared to three-, four-, and five-year-olds that are presented during morning hours so that the kindergarten teacher can include them in her daily planning. These programs are repeated in the late afternoons for home viewing. A new series of programs depicting daily problems with children in family situations is also presented on a dual time slot, both evenings and late afternoons. This series was supplemented with radio call-in programs and regular, organized weekly parent groups throughout the country.

Funds for these special projects geared to social betterment are made available by the government. Support for other educational projects in early childhood are available through private, philanthropic funds.

FUTURE TRENDS

In the last decade, there has been increasing interest and attention given to the importance of the very early years. This is manifested clearly in several newer developments: (1) The Ministry of Education and Culture has made public its intention to become increasingly involved with the ongoing services for children from birth to three years. The responsibility for the care of these children has hitherto been limited to the Ministry of Social Welfare and the philanthropic organizations. (2) New programs for developing senior personnel concerned with the needs of early childhood have been developed by the Ministry of Education and Culture and the Hebrew University in Jerusalem (Rosenthal, 1980). (3) There is a high probability that legislation currently under consideration will make preschools for three- and four-year-olds part of the formal framework of the free and compulsory educational system. (4) For the first time in the long history of early child care and education in Israel, professionals involved with young children have organized to form the Israel Association for Early Childhood.

Early child care and education is an intrinsic and integral part of the Israeli social system. It is well rooted all over the country and in all settings. Looking ahead, the focus is gradually shifting from legitimacy and numbers to standards and quality.

REFERENCES

Egozi, M. & Bielecky, P. Ma-arechet Hachinuch Be-rei Hamisparim (A Statistical View of the Education System) 1980, Ministry of Education and Culture, Jerusalem.

Encyclopaedia Judaica, 1971. Keter Pub., Jerusalem, Vol. 10, p. 963.

Kindergarten Attendance Among Ages 2-4 (Jewish Population) January-March 1978, Ministry of Education and Culture, The Central Bureau of Statistics, 97, July, 1979.

Lombard, A. *Success Begins at Home*, 1981, D.C. Heath & Co., Lexington.

Ministry of Education and Culture, Letochnit ha-avoda began hayeladim. (Work programs for kindergartens.) Handbook 2, Jerusalem, 1966.

Naftali, N. Hashita ha-intensivit: Hanachot vegishot. (The intensive system: underlying assumptions and approaches.) The Ministry of Education and Culture, Department of Supervision of Kindergartens, January, 1968.

Nir, N., Lash, I. & Jiv, T. 1973, "Kvutzot Diun Morim-Horim" (Teacher-Parent Discussion Groups), KEDMA Research Report 174, Pub. 525, April 1973, Ruth Bressler Educational Research Center, Jerusalem.

Rosenthal, Miriam. "Developing Leadership for Integrated Early Childhood Programs in Israel," *Young Children*, March 1980.

Statistical Abstracts of Israel, 1980, 31, Central Bureau of Statistics, Jerusalem.

Statistical Abstracts of Israel, 1980-81, 32.

Chapter 3

PRESCHOOL EDUCATION IN INDIA

GEETA R. LALL and SUSHILA PODDAR

INTRODUCTION

UNTIL about twenty-five years ago, the connection between education and national development had received relatively little public attention in India. However, in recent years, factors such as the spectacular impact of Soviet technological achievements, the belated recognition of the needs of underdeveloped societies for educated manpower as well as capital investment, and studies that show the relevance of education to the economic health of a country have combined to give a new emphasis to the school as a factor in economic and social development (Laska, 1968).

This new emphasis is very apparent in India. It can be observed that the educational system of India reflects both its ancient culture and its recent awakening. In the past, education was for the select few. Today, India's educators and political leaders strive not only to educate the majority but also to adapt education to the country's social needs (Haggerty, 1969).

In trying to achieve this type of universal education, great consideration has been given to preschool education. Preschools are needed and are essential for lower-, middle-, and poorer-class families that are unable to provide a meaningful learning situation for their children. Nursery schools with suitable facilities and equipment are found in large cities. Similar schools need to be opened in rural areas so that all children have the opportunity of attending preschool.

In the case of tribal and backward areas, there is little or no opportunity for a child to receive any training at home because all the adult members of the family work from dawn until dusk. In addition to this, these people can hardly provide the toys or educational materials that a child needs for playing or learning. These children have the natural environment about them and are free to do whatever they like. This freedom, however, does not compensate for the guidance and facilities that a preschool can provide.

It is intriguing to note that in 1972, 17 percent of India's 540 million population were of preschool age. Adding fifteen million each year to the preschool roster, there are now approximately 190 million children of preschool age. This is quite a large number, and the big question is how these children can be reached. A second factor also looms quite large—the poverty that exists. In some western countries, the disadvantaged minority is evident, but in India it is the disadvantaged majority. With these two enormous disadvantages, one would expect that the odds against preschool education would be great. It would also be reasonable to assume that very little was being done about preschool education in India. However, some people believe that "India has potentially one of the best developed systems of preschool education in the world" (Iredale, 1975).

Philosophy of E.C.E.

Despite its huge population, India has adopted the concept of basic education for all (Hagerty, 1969). The philosophy embodied in this concept may be summarized as follows: The education formerly available to Indians weaned them away from their cultural and physical environment and encouraged them to leave their villages for Western-oriented urban centers; the education that should be available would help them both to strengthen the unique aspects of India's age long culture and also to improve tangibly their own physical and social environment (Haggerty, 1969).

Many Indian educators and government officials hold that although there may be different methods to get children involved in the learning process, the method used in their country must be distinctively Indian. It should be relevant to the Indian way of life.

Mahatma Gandhi held to a philosophy that today is prevalent among Indian educators. He believed that the preschool system should be an integral part of the community, involving parents and children, with children under seven years of age included in pre-basic education. His major goal was to take preschool education out of the elite circles and make it available as a right of the masses by developing a sound, inexpensive preschool program, one that involved the students in learning activities as well as the dignity of work. Although many educators have worked towards this philosophy, the full impact of the program has not really caught on, and preschool educators in India still find themselves adhering to foreign philosophies while grappling to define their own.

Of the foreign philosophies prevalent in India, the philosophies of Montessori and Froebel are the most widespread. During the 1940s, Maria Montessori lived in India where she developed the Montessori Methods of Preschool Education, which survives to this day. Friedrich Wilhelm August Froebel developed his methods of preschool education in Blackenberg, Germany, in 1837, and his philosophy and methodology were brought to India by missionaries in the early twentieth century. His methodology and philosophy both continue their influence on Indian preschool educational programs. Maria Montessori and Friedrich Froebel have greatly influenced the course of preschool educational trends and philosophies in India.

Since independence was gained in 1947, great emphasis was placed on the different indigenous philosophies of education for the young nation. Any form of foreign educational pattern, methodology, and philosophy received a temporary setback. Montessori's and Froebel's methods were no exception. Nevertheless, in time, the popularity of these two methods gained momentum. In recent years, Montessori's methods appear to be favored over the methods of Froebel.

Historical Development of E.C.E.

Early childhood education programs are inventions of the past one and a half centuries (Spodek, 1973). It is correct to say that India's achievement in this area has been due to this tradition of preschool. During the 1940s, India went through major changes because of World War II and her newly gained independence. There were several events that took place in the country. One of the most important events was the development of a suitable preschool program for Indian preschool children (Poddar, 1975).

In 1944, the preindependent Government of India appointed the Sergeant Committee, which issued its first document on preschool education. It urged that the states establish "free attractive preschool in order to make the most of this very impressionable, plastic, educationally important period in a child's life" (Tape). No major action was taken by the government, so most of the effort in the preschool sector was voluntary.

ORGANIZATION AND ADMINISTRATION OF E.C.E. PROGRAMS

In India, the balwadis (preschools) are subjected to a different administrative hierarchy than that of the elementary, middle, and high schools. The Ministry of Education does not control the balwadis. Instead, they are controlled by the Central Welfare Board, whose responsibility it is to develop preprimary education in the country as part of family and child welfare schemes. This administrative pattern runs counter to the Education Commision of 1966, which propounded "a close liaison between education and social welfare, together with a pre-primary center within state Institutes of Education" (Iredale, 1968).

The administrative structure of the preschools is well outlined. It depicts the liaison that is necessary for effective supervision. Iredale, commenting on its administrative structure, states:

> Preschool education, while controlled by the Director of Social Welfare in the State (and usually by a specialist child welfare officer reporting directly to him), is administered at the block level by an extension officer, known as a mukhya sevika (responsible for between twenty-four and sixty villages or their equivalent), below whom are usually two (sometimes five) gram sevikas, with the balsevika, the individual pre-school 'teacher' or 'organizer' forming the base of the pyramid. The system provides, in principle, the kind of administrative structure necessary for the proper supervision and inservice encouragement of the teacher (Iredale, 1968).

The various approaches to the problem of preschool education has led to the development of different types of organizations and programs (Naik, 1974). These include the Montessori system, the Froebelian Schools, Minimum-Standard preschools, Mobile Creches for working mothers' children, and Laboratory preschools.

We shall now consider them independently so as to ascertain their importance in the historical development and structure of preschools in India.

The Montessori System. The system had a unique impact in India because of Maria Montessori's prolonged and influential stay in that country. The person responsible for her visit was Annie Bessent—an Irish radical socialist who made India her home. When she died in 1933, her associates in Madras set up a school in her memory. Montessori set up a model preschool in Madras. Due to its impact and popularity, especially among the middle and upper classes of the society, the system was recognized by the Government in 1947 (Tape).

Montessori holds that "the role of the school is to create an environment that will teach the child, with a minimum of adult intervention. The inner power of the child is utilized for his instruction. The child has great powers of observation even during infancy. The program of the school builds upon these powers of observation. Educational programs should begin with objects that appeal to the child's senses" (Spodek, 1973).

Today many of these schools exist in India. Some have made changes and adaptations while others are very orthodox and stick to the letter of the program. In spite of its apparent success many Indian educators hold that this is not the ideal for India (Tape).

The Froebelian Kindergarten. The philosophy and methodology of the Froebelian Kindergarten was introduced in India by missionaries in the early twentieth century (Poddar, 1975). Froebel prescribes to a permissive education. Spodek (1973) commenting on this philosophy states that "education should follow development, guarding and protecting the child. It should not direct, determine, or interfere. Such an education should be based upon freedom and self-determination. It should grow out of the child's free will rather than be imposed from the outside."

Looking at India then with its caste system, one can understand why this system succeeded.

The Montessori and Froebelian systems of preschool education can be considered the forerunners of existing programs. However, new emphasis is not being placed on services to the preschool group from the viewpoint of improving the health and productivity of the population as a whole and for preparing a strong base for universal primary education. Some states have taken innovative approaches. Those adopted by Tamil Nadu and Maharshtra are particularly interesting.

The Minimum-Standard Preschool. These grew out of a Government preschool report in 1963-64. The aim was to cope with the needs of children by creating good, inexpensive education so that a large number of children could benefit (Tape). Any village where the community is prepared to employ a child-care worker and pay her a salary of about twenty rupees per month may conduct a preschool center. On an average, 130 to 140 children attend the preschool, and midday meals are supplied to about 800 preschools with assistance from CARE. Many rural areas are benefiting from this program (Naik, 1974).

Naik (1974), commenting on the assets of the program, states:

"The employment of a literate rural woman to conduct the preschool is the major innovative feature of this program. Her main task is to help the children stay clean, give them their midday meal and engage them in organized play activities; in addition she tells them stories and teaches songs. Much of her work takes the form of baby-sitting. Even this must be considered as a significant improvement in the sense that if she did not give them any attention, the children would have been unable to stay clean or become socialized, nor would they have been able to eat a proper midday meal. Since the cost of the programme is low and since each centre provides a job for a needy and able village woman the programme is likely to spread rapidly" (p. 15).

Several states are trying this system of preschool, and it seems to be most popular and successful in Madras where there are hundreds of schools.

Mobile Creches for Working Mothers' Children. They are regarded as style setters for the future. Their development is considered important because they act as day care centers.

This program was first introduced by the government, which passed a law stating that a creche must be erected at every construction site. The law was not enforced. A few years later, a Gandhian by the name of M. Mahadaven committed her life to alleviate the conditions at the lower economic level. The program she introduced was a volunteer one in which volunteers raised money and administered the program. The only persons paid a salary were teachers, creche workers, and the medical staff. This program demonstrated to the community and to observers from other areas that it was possible to run a good creche and to involve the community in its program (Tape).

Laboratory Preschools. There are two dozen Laboratory preschools attached to universities. This can be considered as a late development in the history of preschools in India. The best known of these Laboratory schools is attached to the University of Baroda. In this preschool, there are eighty children from different economic classes. The school offers a one year course in preschool education and it is used for observation, practice teaching, and research (Tape).

The Extent of E.C.E. Programs

It is very much in evidence that the government of India is concerned that preschool education should be available to all. In 1972, the Minister of Education and Development of Social Welfare stated that "social justice demands attention to the preschool child because the first five years are crucial for all forms of development. The effects of the deprived or abundant environment are most telling at this stage. Investment in human resource development proves a waste if the foundations have been neglected" (Tape).

It is very difficult to give in detail the extent of E.C.E. programs in India. This is due to the diversity of the agencies running both the schools and the teachers' training programs. Anyhow, Roger Iredale gives us some information when he writes that

> Between 1951 and 1966 the known enrollment in mainly urban preprimary schools in the country rose from 28,000 to 250,000 (though these figures must be viewed as vague estimates), while in 1966 the number of children enrolled in rural balwadis was claimed to be 6,000,000

(Report of the Education Commission, 1964-66, p. 149). By 1974 the number of children benefitting from nutrition schemes at feeding centers and balwadis all over the country amounted to nearly four million, of which approximately 1,800,000 were in tribal areas, and 1,700,000 in urban areas. (India, A Reference Annual 1974, Govt. of India, p. 93). (Iredale, 1968, p. 231)

With the availability of more teachers and versatile, organized supervisors, it is believed that the preschool program will touch all of India. It will become a savior of many children, especially those in rural areas, who become dropouts because they have to become domestic baby-sitters while the parents work. Roger Iredale puts it succinctly when he states that "in many ways the preschool system, already developed but not yet ossified, really does represent the cornerstone of the whole educational system" (Iredale, 1968, p. 235).

India is trying many different methods to reach its children of preschool age. There is no doubt that with its present momentum preschools will soon be as common as primary schools in India.

Financing of E.C.E. Program

Financing preschool education in India has been a great challenge. The variety of programs offered, the teeming numbers of preschoolers, and the paucity of resources have made it difficult to allocate the required finances needed to carry out or improve on available programs. The government plays its part by allocating a specified amount on a yearly or on a Five-Year Plan to balwadis and special pilot projects. The money that is allocated is not only used for education, but also for child welfare, which is included in India's preschool programs.

Haggerty (1969), commenting on the government's contribution to preschool education states, "In the Third Five-Year Plan, the Federal Government provided 6 million dollars for strengthening balwadis and for intensive pilot projects for child welfare. At the same time, the States initiated several model preprimary schools at various educationally strategic centers."

Other methods of financing preschool programs are contributions from the community and foreign programs such as CARE.

CURRICULUM IN E.C.E. PROGRAMS

The influence of Montessori and Froebel is so widespread in India that it will be worthwhile at this point to examine their methods and philosophies and see how they permeate the curriculum in preschool programs.

The people of India have run their balwadis for many years. They have adapted their activities to suit the conditions of life in India. They have developed activities that they found necessary and beneficial. For economic reasons they have made use of indigenous items such as waste paper and local material. They have encouraged folk art and folk literature and have drawn the adult population of their area into their cultural activities.

One cannot say whether the method is strictly Montessorian or Froebelian. Since Dr. Montessori's method is understood through her books and from what was found in her schools in India, it can be said that the people are very well impressed by the four principles she introduced in child education and by the ingenious material she evolved for sensory training, language study, and mathematics.

The four principles she initiated, "freedom," "spontaneity," "auto-education," and "auto-correction," were based on modern psychology and were revolutionary in the field of education (Spodek, 1967). She freed children from the shackles of timetables, from teacher's teaching, from learning through force and rigid discipline, from the fear of punishments, insults, and humiliation, and from unhealthy bribes. Indians have studied her methods for some time, and their faith in them is strengthened and stabilized.

Dr. Montessori gave importance to the child. She paid careful attention to the physical and psychological needs of children. She stressed the point that the young child be given complete freedom. She also emphasized that the environment must be compatible with the culture of the community and nation. Dr. Montessori borrowed from the principles of Rousseau, Pestalozzi, and Froebel, modified them to suit Indian standards of living, and evolved her own principles for teaching young children. She insisted that it was the teacher's duty to guide the children while keeping herself in the background. Children in her school were to be brought into direct contact with the didactic materials and not with the teacher. Dr. Montessori had the opinion that the child has an innate potential to learn and to acquire knowledge. When he is left alone without the interference of the adult, the teacher, he will learn better and his learning will be more effective. She emphasized that the child's senses should be involved in the learning process. This gave importance to the sense training and self-correction. Individualized instruction is another important principle that Dr. Montessori introduced in her school (Montessori, 1954).

The Montessori program seems to be widely accepted in India. Her concept of the child and the development and environmental predispositions for learning seemed to woo the upper classes to her schools. Her daily program has little structure and the child is given the freedom to work at self-chosen tasks in an attractive environment.

The school's curriculum includes exercises in practical life, muscular education, education of the senses, intellectual education, language education and the teaching of reading, writing, and numeration. Nature study, gardening, and handicraft activities are also part of the program and are incorporated when possible (Spodek, 1973).

Most of these schools are located in well kept buildings; varied types of didactic, self-correcting materials are located at strategic points in open areas so that the child can move freely from one project to another as his interest dictates.

Froebel's Principles of Education

According to Froebel the aim of education was not to make the mind master of the three R's. He wrote, "The essential business of school is not so much to communicate a variety and multiplicity of facts as to give prominence to the ever-living unity that is in all things . . . . Human education requires the knowledge and appreciation of the intimate unity of the three; the school and we ourselves are lost in the fallacies of bottomless, self-provoking diversity" (Muralidharan, 1968).

So the aim of education is to enable the child to realize unity in diversity.

Froebel believed that the school is to be a social laboratory where the children get training in primary virtues such as cooperation, sympathy, fellow feelings, and responsibility. In other words, the school is a miniature society of its own.

Play is the basis of education according to Froebel. The child expresses himself best in play, but at the same time, learns much that would otherwise tax his memory.

Froebel believed that occupations in kindergarten have changed the face of the modern methods of teaching. Learning by doing, dramatics, work experience, and self-expression are all hidden in this scheme of education. Inclusion of manual work is a great influence on the minds of the teachers.

He emphasized the principle of proceeding from concrete to abstract. The provision of gifts in the first place of the scheme is based on it. It provides sensory training to the child.

To provide activities, Froebel devised suitable material known as gifts. The gifts suggested some form of activity, and occupations are the activities suggested by the gifts. These have been carefully graded. The order of the gift was devised in such a way that it led the child from the activities and thoughts of one stage to those of another.

His emphasis on nature study and gardening has fulfilled a long felt need of children for observation and love of the world in which they live. He believed that songs, gestures, and construction should be the chief means for stimulating the imagination of the child. He also believed that the child should be educated in a free atmosphere. Freedom means obedience to self-imposed law. The sum and substance of the educational aim, according to Froebel, is the realization of the law of unity through the development of one's mind in accordance with its own inner law and through being self-active in a free and social atmosphere.

Freedom is the core of this method. Play and joy will be typical of such an atmosphere. There are no books in it. Storing of knowledge is not required in it. Expression is the key of this method. The learning process is activity centered. It is imparted in three ways, through songs, through movements, and through construction. All these activities will be well connected as a unit. Play will be the pivot of the whole process. Everything is experienced through songs. Children express themselves in creative activities such as paper construction or the use of cardboard or wooden blocks.

Thus, creative and concrete means are adopted to stimulate mental activity on the part of children. They are trained intellectually, physically, and emotionally. The teacher's job is to select songs, to devise plays and games, to show pictures, and to arrange activities.

Froebel gave importance to manual work because it provided a concrete form of repression of ideas. He attached spiritual importance to manual work. Froebel's demand for the inclusion of manual work in the school curriculum was based on this legalistic concept of work. Manual work was a necessary condition for the realization of the pupil's personality; through it he comes to find himself.

According to him the main purpose of education is all round development. He divided the curriculum in four parts:
1. Religion and religious instruction.
2. Natural science and mathematics.
3. Language.
4. Art and objects of art.

Froebel believed that nature study would create a sense of wonder and admiration in the minds of the children for works of God. Nature study would result in religious upliftment and spiritual insight. Therefore, the child must have knowledge about all the important facts of nature.

Thus the period of childhood is characterized as predominantly that of life for the mere sake of living, for making internal external; also, childhood is predominantly the period for learning, for making the external internal.

The Frobelian program is based on his idealistic philosophy of unity in diversity. He viewed knowledge as being achieved through the grasp of symbols. The basic elements of his curriculum are (1) the gifts that consist of ten manipulative materials to be used by children in a preschool manner, (2) the occupations that deal with solids, surfaces, lines, points, and constructions, (3) games and songs, (4) nature study, and (5) work in language and arithmetic (Spodek, 1973).

The facilities of the Froebelian program are adequate. Many of the schools are well equipped with materials, games, and space for play and socialization. The buildings are well-kept and are indicative of the society that uses it.

Although the influence of Montessori and Froebel is so wide-spread, the facilities and programs in other preschool organizations should also be mentioned.

The Minimum-Standard Preschool has a very unusual central factor—that is, feeding of children and expectant mothers. This program is concerned with the total welfare of the child because of the high death rate between birth and age six. Other aspects of the program are physical activity, walking, hopping, running, and story telling. Toys and equipment are very minimal. Emphasis is placed on using the objects on hand such as sticks, stones, and leaves for the teaching of language and arithmetic.

These schools meet in very informal places: under a tree, in an open courtyard, or on the verandah of a school (Tape).

Basic education that embodies a distinctive Indian approach consists of and includes personal hygiene, morning prayer, reading, counting, and a choice of some special activity such as spinning or gardening. These schools have no special equipment—everyday occurrences are utilized. For example, vegetable gardening helps the child learn proper food habits, nutrition value, and facts on soil and water (Tape).

The program at the Mobile creche is suited to the needs of that community which consists mainly of migrant workers. A daily program starts with a woman from the creche fetching the children from their homes and bringing them to the temporary classroom on the construction site. There she feeds them, washes them, gives them a snack, and works with them according to their age. For the younger kids, she provides recreation and activity, and for the older kids, she starts with programs that promote literacy. At intervals or break-time, mothers come to the site and either breast-feed their kids or keep an eye on them.

The facilities for this type of program are improvised. The classroom could be a temporary shed, or an unfinished part of the building may be used. There is little or no sanitation at these sites and workers at the creche have to be innovative as they provide for the total care of the children (Tape).

The Laboratory preschools attached to universities carry a well organized program. Its emphasis is on creative activity and individual development. Because these schools are used for observation, practice teaching, and research, its program is greatly varied and the trend is modern and progressive.

These schools are well housed, well staffed, and well equipped. There is little or nothing missing from these programs (Tape).

Teacher Training

Training for preschool teachers in India takes place at different levels. There are many training institutions that provide for balwadi teachers. "One main trainer is the India Council for Child Welfare (a recognized nongovernmental organization), which has eleven centers in various states and which gives about 600 women every year an eleven month certificate course" (Iredale, 1968).

Some teachers are trained in Rural Extension Training Centers, often under some specific scheme such as the Integrated Child Development Scheme, which emanated from New Delhi in 1973-74. In addition, there is a middle school where eighth grade or high school girls are given crash training or job orientation courses of two to three months (Iredale, 1968).

Four states offer private Froebelian nursery training programs that run for one year. They borrow many concepts from other systems, especially if the idea involves formal training (Tape).

The Association of Montessori National in India conducts training courses in different parts of the country. These programs are set up mainly by Montessori disciples. The program is taught for two years, and students are put through a syllabus and examination, that is, in most states, set and administered by the State Board of Education. This is a very rigorous program and is the most recognized qualification in many states (Iredale, 1968).

In India, teachers are selected mainly on a basis of academic qualification rather than experience. The vast majority of India's teachers and administrators hold university degrees. It is obvious that these qualified teachers do not teach in preschools; they prefer to teach at the higher levels. Thus, the teacher trainers in this area do not have preschool experience and teach their trainees on a very theoretical basis, which is a draw-back in the field of preschool education (Iredale, 1968).

Another barrier to successful administration is the supervisory system. In the preschool system, the supervisor and his deputy act as a "snooper" whose main interest is that of checking the attendance registers, auditing the school accounts, and making sure that the supplies and food allotments are adequately accounted for instead of giving emphasis to effective guidance and the proper running of the schools. Iredale (1968), in a reference to the *Pre-primary Institutions—Their Supervision: A Handbook for Supervisory Staff,* stresses this problem by quoting, "It may be mentioned that one of the missing links of preprimary education programmes would appear to be the absence of trained supervisory staff who are able to provide effective guidance to the pre-school teachers regarding the proper maintenance and running of the pre-schools (p. 5)."

CONCLUSION

Preschool education in India has made giant steps since its independence in 1947. Although many educators still adhere to the old traditions, some have implemented unconventional methods that are more beneficial to preschoolers.

The challenge of educating the masses, using available resources, has been met. The Minimum-Standard preschool and the mobile creche preschool demonstrates the ingenuity and foresight of those who comprehend the goals of preschool education as defined by their culture.

In addition to these, there are a large number of kindergarten and Montessori schools, especially in urban areas. The philosophies of Froebel and Montessori appear to be widespread; in recent years, Montessori's methods seemed to be favored over those of Froebel's.

Preschool education is not stagnating. It seems to be growing just as fast as, or even faster than, that of many other developed countries. The total welfare of the child is important. The nutritional needs of the child are viewed as one of the greatest avenues through which a preschool child can benefit. The community has been involved in pilot projects, thus implementing one of the modern principles of total involvement.

Much still needs to be done for preschool education in India. Adequately trained staff and administrators need to be found and utilized. Teachers need practical training in addition to their theoretical backgrounds so that they may be able to deal with situations which are not incorporated in textbooks. Efficient and adequate administration is needed so that teachers may obtain the direction needed to guide their students into maximizing their potentialities.

Despite these difficulties, preschool education in India seems to be moving in the right direction. The goal is for all children from birth to six years old to be involved in a meaningful, beneficial form of education.

REFERENCES

Flaming, Daniel: *Schools with a Message in India*. London, Oxford University Press, 1921.

Haggerty, William: *Higher and Professional Education in India*. Washington, U.S. Government Printing Office, 1969.

Iredale, Roger: *Pre-school Education in India*. New York, Teachers College Press, 1968.

Laska, John: *Planning and Educational Development in India*. New York, Teachers College Press, 1968.

Montessori, Maria: *The Discovery of the Child*. India, Kalakshetra Publications, 1952.

Montessori, Maria: *The Discovery of the Child*. Madras, Kalakshetra Publications, 1951.

Muralidharan, R.: *The System of Pre-School Education in India*. Delhi, Indian Association for Preschool Education, 1968.

Poddar, Sushila: *A Comparison of Froebel Kindergarten Pre-School Education in India*. Berrien Springs, Michigan, Andrews University, 1975.

Spodek, Bernard: *Early Childhood Education*. Englewood Cliffs, New Jersey, Prentice-Hall, Inc., 1973.

Spodek, Bernard: *Pre-School Education in India*. Delhi, Indian Association for Pre-School Education, 1967.

Spodek, Bernard: *Sourcebook for Pre-School Education*. Baroda, Indian Association for Pre-School Education. 1972.

Tape: *Early Childhood Education. International India*. S. Anandalashymy, interviewed by James L. Hymes Jr. Childhood Resources, Inc., 1973.

Chapter 4

EARLY CHILDHOOD EDUCATION IN JAPAN

MASAKO SHOJI

INTRODUCTION

AT the time of the Meiji Restoration (1868), Japan realized that education was most important in its aim to become modernized. The Meiji Government sent many officials and scholars to Europe and America in order to examine science, industry, technology, and the educational system. Upon his return from America, Tanaka Fujimaro*, Minister of Education, proposed the establishment of a national kindergarten. The first one, modeled after the American schools, was opened in 1876 at the Tokyo Women's Normal School. Froebel's gifts, songs, and plays were taught, even though the teachers had no knowledge of his principles relating to early childhood education.

In the years that followed, other private kindergartens were established, but both the government and society became disinterested in these institutions. After World War II, a new educational system from America was introduced. Thus, when studies on education, child psychology, and educational sociology were promoted the general public began to realize the importance of early childhood education.

---

*Japanese names are written in the traditional style, that is, last name first, and first name last.

48

As the number of working mothers increased, day nurseries became necessary and popular. Unfortunately though, there were insufficient qualified teachers and nurses. Recently, many teachers and nurses have been going to both Europe and America to examine and study early childhood education in order to improve this area of education in Japan.

PHILOSOPHY OF EARLY CHILDHOOD
EDUCATION IN JAPAN

Scholars Urge Importance of Early Childhood Education

Nakae Toju (1608-1648) said that "Since children copy their parents and nurses, the adults [should] try to improve themselves." He believed that the aim of early childhood education was to cultivate a child's mind to possess the virtues of Buddha.

Yamaga Soko (1622-1685) suggested that "when children are still small, their life should be centered in plays. . . . Etiquette should be taught in everyday life."

In his book *Wazokudojikun*, Kaibara Ekiken (1630-1714) presented the most systematic philosophy of early childhood education. He believed that education should begin as early as possible and that children ought to be taught according to their age and nature, being trained in both mind and body. He also stressed the importance of early discipline at home and warned against the danger of doting, overprotective parents.

Sato Nobujiro (1769-1850) was the first to suggest and plan for nursing facilities for infants. He envisioned two phases: the first for babies of the poor, where they would be cared for until four or five years old. Then they would be sent to the second facility where nurses and old people could take care of them at the government's expense. However, his plans were not realized.

Development of Basic Aims of Kindergarten Education

The first kindergarten had the following objectives: to develop the intellect, cultivate mind and body, assist in social growth, and cultivate moral character.

In "The Essentials of Nurture" issued in 1882, the aim was to develop body, mind, and moral character in order to prepare children for the elementary school.

The "Kindergarten Law" of 1926 went one step further in that it aimed at also supplementing home education.

Later, with the progress of war during the Showa Era, the aim of kindergarten education became nationalistic and militaristic.

After World War II and the promulgation of the new Constitution a new emphasis was placed on educating for happiness and peace.

HISTORICAL DEVELOPMENT OF EARLY CHILDHOOD EDUCATION IN JAPAN

Historical Development of the Kindergarten

The Meiji Era (1868-1911). The first kindergarten, established by the Japanese government in 1876, was attached to the Tokyo Women's Normal School. The aims of this institution were to develop natural talent, cultivate the mind, enhance health, teach the art of association with others, and encourage mastery of good speech habits and behavior patterns.

Generally, children from three to five years of age were admitted. They were divided according to age: three-, four-, and five-year-olds, with about forty in each class. They spent about four hours per day at school.

According to the 1877 annual report of the Ministry of Education, the areas taught were life, beauty, and knowledge. Using Froebel's kindergarten methods, the teachers covered subjects such as playing with five-colored balls, pasting up paper, drawing, working with chopsticks, singing, understanding of triangles, paper cutting, paper folding, etc.

As yet no governmental law concerning kindergartens had been passed, but the regulations of the first school were accepted and followed by other new institutions, two of which were built in 1879, one in Osaka and the other in Kagoshima. Two years later certain regulations pertaining to kindergartens were drawn up. In order to receive permission to establish such a school, the aims of the institution, location, curriculum, regulations, holidays, salary scale, a sketch of the building, etc. had to be submitted to either the Minister of Education (for a national school) or to the governor of the prefecture (for a local public or private one).

Around this time a depression hit Japan, and the Minister of Education decided to build more kindergartens so that children of any age could be cared for while both parents worked. Thus, smaller and cheaper schools were built, serving both an educational and a social welfare purpose.

Both in 1889 and 1890, regulations were issued that served to clarify the aims of kindergarten education. Gradually the number of schools increased, and by 1897 there were fourteen national kindergartens as well as 153 local public and fifty-five private ones with a total enrollment of 20,000.

As kindergarten education began to spread across the nation, it became increasingly apparent that the existing regulations were inadequate to meet current situations. Thus, at the proposal of the Froebel Association, the Ministry of Education enacted "Regulations for Kindergarten Education, and for its Facilities and Equipment" in June, 1899. This law regulated school age, school hours, size of enrollment, building facilities, curriculum, equipment, and the fundamentals of education.

The Taisho Era (1912-1926). In April 1926, the Ministry of Education passed the "Kindergarten Act," based on the 1899 law, and the "Kindergarten Act Enforcement Regulations" to meet current demands. By now there were 1,066 schools with a total enrollment of about 100,000. Kindergartens were now being established at a rapid rate with the overwhelming majority situated in urban areas.

The First Period of the Showa Era (1926-1945). After World War I, nationalism was gradually emphasized in all education. Kindergarten education tried at first to retain its liberal system but, with the approach of a quasi-wartime order, was obliged to become nationalistic in its aims and curriculum.

During the course of the Second World War, many kindergarten buildings were destroyed. Classes were stopped, and the remaining schools were used as wartime day nurseries to supplement the regular nursery schools.

Historical Development of the Day Nursery

Origins and Purpose. When the day nursery was first started, it was called "the public nursery" or "the children's home."

Akazawa Kaneni and his wife operated the Seishu School in Niigata, which attracted students primarily from the poorer class. These pupils had to bring their little brothers and sisters to school to care for them and found it rather difficult to study at the same time. To solve the problem, Mrs. Akazawa decided to care for the children during classtime. Later, the Akazawas extended this free service to the neighborhood children of widows and widowers. Thus began Japan's first day nursery in 1890.

Later in 1894 another nursery was opened in the Dainippon Spinning Company to care for the infants of the mothers working there, and in 1899 Noguchi Yukako, with the help of a missionary, Miss Denton, opened the Futaba Yochien in a slum area in Tokyo. Eighty years later this institution still exists and is called the Futaba Day Nursery.

Wartime Day Nurseries. In 1905, the Aizawa Children's Home was established in Yokohama by Niromiya Waka to serve the families bereaved during the Russo-Japanese War; another one was opened by the Women's Service in Kobe. The next year, several additional day nurseries were organized.

As a result of the postwar depression and the 1918 Rice Riot, the Ministry of Home Affairs decided to ease the social unrest by building several day nurseries to care for the preschool children of working families. Previously, during the Meiji Era, all the day nurseries had been built and supported by private organizations or philanthropists, but from 1919 onwards, public day nurseries were organized, the first one being opened in Osaka. By 1921, there were 100 nurseries nationwide.

Day Nursery Policies. The day nursery, based on the curriculum of the kindergarten, had the primary aim of caring for the children of working guardians. It was only a matter of secondary importance to place them in an improved environment where they could receive a good mental and physical education. Also, with no minimum standard qualifications indicated, anybody could work at one of these institutions.

In 1947, the day nursery and the kindergarten were given a legal base. As a result of the School Education Law, the kindergarten was considered a preschooling facility, whereas the Child Welfare Law classified the day nursery as a welfare facility. Thus, because of these two laws the system of preschool education was divided.

EXTENT OF EARLY CHILDHOOD EDUCATION IN JAPAN

The Kindergarten

In 1945 at the close of the war, education in Japan changed completely from a militaristic to a democratic type. Two years later, a series of laws concerning education was passed. Among these was the School Education Law, which included several articles pertaining to kindergarten education. Children from three to elementary school age were to be taught cooperation, self-reliance, correct language, creative expression, social interaction, etc.

Upon realizing that the basic personality patterns are shaped during the early years of life, the Ministry of Education undertook a survey to assess the strength of its early childhood education program. It found that of all the 1948 first-graders, only 7 percent had received kindergarten education. Probably this was partly due to the fact that the number of kindergartens was 8.5 percent of the number of elementary schools. More than 54 percent of these preschool institutions were private. Thus, with the realization of the importance of preschool education, it was urged that national and public institutions take more responsibility for kindergarten education.

Parents became so eager to send their children to kindergarten that often two to three times the number of children who could enter would turn up for enrollment. Many of those who could not enter the kindergarten then went to day nurseries. So much so that out of 248,775 attending day nurseries in 1950, 111,115 (44.7%) did not need the protection of the Child Welfare Act.

In 1954, the Ministry of Education issued the revised Essentials of Kindergarten Education. The "Seven Year Plan to Promote Kindergarten Education" aimed at increasing preschool training so that by 1970 at least 60 percent of first-graders would have attended kindergarten.

The statistics of the thirteen years (1965-1977) show an encouraging trend. In 1965, only 44.2 percent of five-year-olds were attending kindergarten, but by 1977 the percentage had increased to 65.1.

At present, the main concerns of Japanese education are compulsory kindergarten education and lowering the compulsory school age. Consequently, a sort of "kindergarten boom" covers all of Japan.

The Day Nursery. The number of day nurseries also constantly increased. There were 312 in 1928, 878 in 1935, and 1495 in 1939. At that point, the Social Undertaking Act was applied to these institutions on a legal control basis only, seeing that there were no laws regulating them. Efforts were made at both the 1935 Eighth Convention of Social Work and the 1937 All Japan Nurture Convention to write an independent day nursery act.

But before the problem could be solved, Japan got involved with a war, first with China and then with the allied forces. As the war expanded, all day nurseries, children's homes, and kindergartens became wartime day nurseries to meet current demands. Thus for a short time, all kinds of children's institutions were unified in order to cooperate with the war policy. After the war, the kindergartens and day nurseries were separately reconstructed with the latter falling under the jurisdiction of the Ministry of Health and Welfare.

The purpose of the day nursery, according to Article 39, Chapter 3 of the Child Welfare Act, is to "nurture the sucklings and infants who lack the proper care at home." This aim has not been realized by most of the nurseries. Nevertheless, there has been a steady increase in enrollment over the past several years, from 18 percent of five-year-olds in 1965, to 25.4 percent in 1977.

Other Facilities and Institutions for Young Children

Besides the kindergarten and the day nursery, other facilities are being built for children: parks, playgrounds, and children's homes. Homes for mothers and children are also being provided to protect any mother who is without a spouse.

Under the Preventive Vaccination Act, various immunizations are given to all infants. Likewise, all infants between three and four years of age must have the Three-year-old Child's Health Check-up. At this time, advice is given on how to prevent diseases and how to improve the child's health.

In 1963, the Ministry of Education began issuing a family education magazine called *The Discipline of Young Children at Home.* A home education class run by the local board of education was organized in 1964 to assist mothers in basic child training. The Central Child Welfare Council is now attempting to assist parents by selecting and recommending good children's books and good radio and television programs for both parents and children.

FINANCING OF EARLY CHILDHOOD EDUCATION IN JAPAN

The Kindergarten

Financing is as follows: the Japanese government finances any national kindergartens and public schools are supported by the local government, whereas private ones are funded by the founders. Since kindergarten education is not compulsory, parents have to pay a tuition fee. This fee differs depending on what kind of institution it is. For example, in 1978 tuition was 2200 yen per month at a national school, 2067 at a public one, and 11,160 at a private institution. The government does give some assistance to private kindergartens. Parents with a low income can also receive some government aid, up to 80,000 yen per year.

The Day Nursery

The local government bears the expense for the day nurseries. Normally parents are expected to pay some tuition, but for low-income families, a part of the fee is exempted, and it is completely waived in the case of families on relief.

Thus, when it comes to financing the day nurseries, the national government foots 80 percent of the bill, the prefectural government 10 percent, and the municipal government 10 percent.

ADMINISTRATION, CURRICULUM, PERSONNEL, AND PHYSICAL FACILITIES OF EARLY CHILDHOOD EDUCATION IN JAPAN

The Kindergarten

Administration. The School Education Law of 1947, issued by the Ministry of Education, provides for the establishment of state, local public, and private kindergartens. Upon approval by the authorities, these institutions are "to bring up preschool infants, provide a suitable environment for them, and thus develop their minds and bodies" (Act 77 of the School Education Law). Infants from three to the elementary school entrance age are permitted to attend.

Curriculum. The Standard for Kindergarten Curriculum gives the following outline of its purposes: to have well-balanced teaching plans with activities appropriately designed by taking into account the difference in age among children, the length of the teaching period, as well as local conditions.

Six subjects are taught:

1. *Health*—To have children develop an interest in various exercises and the habits and attitudes necessary for a sound, healthy life.

2. *Social Studies*—To encourage children to become interested in their immediate social affairs and to develop desirable habits and attitudes in both private and social life.

3. *Nature*—To acquaint and familiarize children with animals, plants, and the immediate phenomena of nature; to encourage them to observe, comment, and handle such phenomena for themselves; to acquire the simple skills needed for daily life; and to take an interest in numbers and figures.

4. *Language*—To improve listening skills so that they will understand words and stories heard; to foster free and correct expression of ideas; and to acquaint them with picturebooks and storytelling so as to enrich their imagination.

5. *Music and rhythm*—To get children to enjoy listening to music; to encourage singing, the playing of instruments, and the free expression of their thoughts and feelings in sound and action.

6. *Drawing and handicrafts*—To develop an interest in the esthetic; to enable them to experience joy in expressing themselves in free drawings and handicrafts.

Besides the above-mentioned activities, athletic meets, picnics, and school excursions to learn about the community also form a part of the curriculum. Several ceremonies and festivals, like Kindergarten Founder's Day, Star Festival, Moon Viewing, Children's Day, Doll Festival, etc., are participated in every year.

Personnel. Under special circumstances, exceptions can be made, but generally a kindergarten needs to be staffed with a director and some teachers, besides perhaps other personnel.

The director, who is in charge of administrative activities and the supervision of the staff, generally needs to have a first-class regular teacher's certificate with more than five years experience in the educational profession in order to hold such a position.

Full-time teachers who are in charge of child care must be in possession of either a bachelor's degree or a junior college diploma. Under special conditions, full-time assistant teachers or part-time teachers may be substituted, but these staff must at least have the Upper Secondary School Diploma.

Each kindergarten should have a head teacher who assists the director. A nursing or assistant nursing teacher and a clerk are also recommended. Each school should also have a physician, a dentist, and a pharmacist.

There needs to be at least one full-time teacher per class, with not more than forty children of the same age enrolled in it.

Physical Facilities and Equipment. The kindergarten should be located in surroundings adequate for the education of infants. As a rule, it should be a single-story building, but in the case of a nonfireproof two-story building, the nursery rooms, playing rooms, and restrooms must be located on the first floor. Adequate facilities for education, health, sanitation, administration, and playing areas should be provided.

Ideally, each school needs to have a teacher's room, a nursery room, a playing room, and a health room. Restrooms are to be furnished with urinals and toilets; one facility for approximately thirty children. A hygienic drinking fountain, besides washing facilities, should be installed.

Sufficient desks, chairs, blackboards, slides, swings, sand playing fields, building blocks, toys, tools for picture-story shows, books, implements for health and hygiene and for breeding animals, and tools for drawing and handicrafts are to be provided as teaching aids. Also recommended are radio sets, projectors, water playing places, washing stands, lunch service equipment, a library, and a conference room.

The Day Nursery

Administration. The Child Welfare Law of 1947, issued by the Ministry of Health and Welfare, provides for the establishment of day nurseries by either the state, prefecture, municipality, or private persons. The municipality or private individuals must receive permission from the governor of the prefecture before opening such an institution. The purpose of these day nurseries is to care for mainly infants under the elementary school entrance age (6) upon the request of their guardians.

Curriculum. The education of those infants in the day nursery who are of the same age as those in the kindergarten should be based upon the "Standard for Kindergarten Curriculum." Otherwise, the Minimum Standards of Child Welfare Institutions apply.

Nursery care includes a regular health examination; a midday nap; a daily check on the complexion, temperature, skin condition, and state of cleanliness of each child upon arrival at the nursery; time for free play, during which music, rhythm, drawing, painting, manual art, nature, social studies, group games, etc., can be enjoyed; and every day at the time of leaving, a check with regard to cleanliness, cuts or wounds, and the condition of clothing with appropriate measures taken.

As in the case of the kindergarten, picnics, school excursions, and several ceremonies and festivals are participated in by the day nurseries. As a rule, the nursery operates eight hours per day.

Personnel. The day nursery must have day nurses and a part-time physician. There should be at least one day nurse for every six babies under three years of age, at least one for every twenty preschool children between three and four years of age, at least one for every thirty preschool children four or more years of age, and never less than two at any single day nursery. Preferably, day nurses should be graduates of the day nurse training institutes designated by the Minister of Health and Welfare or other corresponding activities.

Physical Facilities and Equipment. Day nurseries must have adequate equipment to provide proper care for infants and to conduct clerical work. For nurseries admitting more than thirty infants, the following is required for infants under two years of age: an infant room of at least 1.69 square meters per child or a crawling-room of at least 3.3 square meters per child, a medical room, a kitchen, and restrooms. Infant or crawling-rooms need to be provided with an indoor slide, a chairswing, a wheeled-walker, and a push-cart. Day nurseries with infants two or more years of age should have a first-floor nursery room or playroom of at least 1.98 square meters per child and an outdoor playground of at least 3.3 square meters per child equipped with sand playing fields, slides, and swings.

Restrooms need to be fitted with sufficient urinals and toilets; one facility for approximately twenty children. The nursery room or playroom should be equipped with musical instruments, blackboards, desks, chairs, building blocks, and picturebooks.

Each day nursery should also be provided with the necessary medical instruments, medicines, bandages, and dressing materials. In the case of a day nursery with fewer than thirty infants, part of the above requirements may be waived.

TEACHER TRAINING FOR EARLY CHILDHOOD EDUCATION IN JAPAN

Facilities for Training Kindergarten Teachers

At first, there were no training schools for kindergarten teachers, and so, carefully selected women were sent to Tokyo to observe the methods used in the first established kindergarten. In 1878, the Ministry of Education passed certain regulations to establish a kindergarten teacher training course at the Tokyo Women's Normal School, where the first kindergarten had been started two years before. Here women over twenty years of age spent one year studying principles of education, physics, zoology, botany, algebra, music, and the gifts theory besides doing some practice teaching.

As a result of the increasing number of kindergarten schools, many more qualified teachers were needed. To fill this need, the Tokoyo Education Association began an institute in 1889, while in the same year, a mission school in Kobe established the Shoei Institute for Kindergarten Teacher Training. By 1892, the Ministry of Education began to show a greater interest in kindergarten teacher training facilities, thus proposing the establishment of such institutions in each prefecture. In addition, regulations were issued stipulating the minimum qualifications for kindergarten staff.

A 1949 survey indicated that 5,526 kindergarten classes were being taught. However, the three national schools and nine private junior colleges that were training teachers could not meet the demand. By March 1971, the situation had changed completely. Of the 26,714 students who received certificates only 8,835 (about 33%) were able to obtain teaching posts in the kindergarten schools.

Training for Day Nursery Attendants

By 1972, the Ministry of Health and Welfare had authorized only thirteen universities, 163 junior colleges, and 105 other schools to have nurse training courses. Thus, with nearly 20,000 day nurseries in operation by 1977, a problem still exists in that about 10 percent of all the nurses are not fully qualified for their jobs.

STRENGTHS AND WEAKNESSES OF EARLY CHILDHOOD EDUCATION IN JAPAN

Current Problems

Several problems can be pointed out in the early childhood education program in Japan.

1. It is difficult to keep contact and arrange curricula between kindergarten schools and day nurseries because the former are controlled by the Ministry of Education and the latter fall under the Ministry of Health and Welfare.

2. Because day nurseries accept children from a few months old to five years, and kindergartens only three- to five-year-olds, children between three and five obtain a different preschool education depending on where they attend.

3. Some private schools have more than forty children per class, and this makes teaching very difficult.

4. Closer contact between the kindergarten and the elementary school is needed, especially concerning curriculum.

5. Some teachers lack the necessary qualifications. Then, of those who have graduated, some have received their certificates

from junior colleges and are not as competent as those who have four-year university degrees.

6. There are not sufficient qualified nurses to staff the day nurseries.

7. As a result of a much higher rate of pay at the public institutions, it is difficult to get teachers for private kindergartens.

Improvements in the Program

The Seven Year Plan of promotion of kindergarten education (1964-1970) was followed by the Ten Year Plan, which began in 1972. In that same year, the Ministry of Education started a new system of financial aid to encourage kindergarten attendance. The plan is to reduce the fees for four- and five-year-olds in accordance with their parent's income, and to have the national and local governments give more financial aid. It was hoped that by 1981, 1,500,000 infants would be enrolled.

In many countries of the world today, the two-year preschool education has come to be considered a necessity. Thus, it appears appropriate to enforce a fundamental policy of establishing a free preschool system without any differences between public or private kindergartens and day nurseries.

SUMMARY

Since the educational system does not always measure up to the high expectations placed upon it, the Japanese are by no means complacent and satisfied with their schools. Intimate involvement and deep interest on the part of the general populace places the schools under constant surveillance and renders them subject to continuous criticism. However, compared to schools in the rest of Asia (and in many Western countries as well), Japanese schools are modern and sophisticated.

Japan's educational system, even with its shortcomings, must be judged effective. Evidence of this is readily at hand in the country's high economic growth rate, expanding industrial society, significant inventions and technological innovations, and important achievements and discoveries in the arts and sciences. It is also observable in the great enthusiasm and eagerness of most students, the dedication of most teachers and their pride in the success of their pupils, and the intense interest of the general populace in culture and recreation.

REFERENCES

Anderson, Ronald S.: *Education in Japan: A Century of Modern Development*, U.S. Dept. of Health, Education and Welfare, Washington, 1975.

Mori Shigeru: The present state and problems of preschool education, *Education in Japan—Journal for Overseas*, Vol. VIII, p. 21-31, 1975.

Shoji Masako: Froebelians in Japan. *Education in Japan—Journal for Overseas*, Vol. I, pp. 54-65, The International Educational Research Institute, Hiroshima University, 1966.

Shoji Masako: Preschool system in Japan. *Education in Japan-Journal for Overseas*, Vol. II, pp. 107-118, 1967.

The Japanese National Committee of O.M.E.P.: *Preschool Education in Japan*, pp. 21-29, 1975.

Related Books in Japanese

Early Childhood Education Association of Japan: *Early Childhood Education and Care in Japan*, Child Honsha Co., Ltd., Tokyo, 1979.

Early Childhood Education Association of Japan: *NIHON HOIKUSHI (or The History of Early Childhood Education in Japan)*, Vol. 1-6: Froebel Inc, Tokyo, 1969-1975.

(Translation from German to Japanese) *Friedrich Frobels gesammelte padagogische Schriften*, Vol. 1-5, Tamagawa University Publisher, Edited by K. Obara and M. Shoji, 1975-1981.

Okada Masaaki: *NIHON NO HOIKUSEIDO (or The System of Early Childhood Education in Japan)*, Froebel Inc., Tokyo, 1970.

Shoji Masako: *YOJIKYOIKU NO GENRI TO HOHO (or the Principles and Methods of Early Childhood Education)*, Froebel Inc., Tokyo, 1969.

The Japanese Association for Early Childhood Education: *NIHONHOIKUSHI (or The History of Early Childhood Education in Japan)*, Vol. 1-6, Froebel Inc., Tokyo, 1969-1975.

The Ministry of Education: *YOCHIENKYOIKU 90 NENSHI (or The History of the Kindergarten for 90 Years)*, HIKARINOKUNI Inc., Osaka, 1969.

Chapter 5

EARLY CHILDHOOD EDUCATION
IN CHINA

GEETA R. LALL and BERNARD M. LALL

INTRODUCTION

CHINA has definite plans for its children. It is a carefully planned society without competing or divergent educational philosophies and methods. The Chinese believe that their children need to be prepared for the working world and for practical life. Hence, every morning the older kindergarten children spend time cleaning the playground, watering plants, washing their towels, and engaging in several other tasks.

In 1977 the director of the Pei Hai Boarding Kindergarten in Peking stated that before the Cultural Revolution the Chinese had pursued a revisionist line, putting the intellectual emphasis first. They had brought up the children to be physically healthy, without paying any attention to ideology. As an example, when children used a tea set, a teacher would discuss their activities to develop their language and intelligence. Nowadays, however, the social significance of the cup made by "aunt" and "uncle" workers would be discussed. This involves drawing attention to the hard work that goes into collecting clay and making cups and saucers. Thus, for these young children education is not divorced from real life experiences and the class struggle.

Even their songs portray this ideology. Here are two examples:

"I'm called the little soldier;
  I want to be a revolutionary even when
    I'm young;
  I want to be a worker, peasant or soldier
    when I grow up."

"My small car is very pretty,
  I toot my horn from time to time;
  I am a small driver for the Revolution!"

HISTORY

During a period of over 2,000 years of continuous civilization, China developed a refined culture. Unfortunately, until this present century higher reaches of this culture have been accessible to only a minority of the population, which included only the bourgeoisie. This system of education that transmitted the cultural heritage of the nation was based upon the conception of a static and hierarchical society. It was centered on the teachings of Confucius, the classical writings, and Chinese history and aimed at maintaining culture rather than developing it.

The ancient Chinese had learned from bamboo books and had obtained moral training and practice in rituals by word of mouth and by example.

When the Communist Party acceded to power in 1949, China had a 20 percent literacy rate. This probably could be attributed to the fact that prior to 1949, schools were available for less than 40 percent of school-age children. The immediate tasks of this new government were to expand the educational system, to abolish illiteracy, and to produce skilled workers and professional personnel sufficient to develop a modern economy.

On October 1, 1951, the Government Administration council of the Central People's Government issued the "Decisions concerning Reform of the Education" system and thereby set up the system of education of the People's Republic of China. This has brought about fundamental reform of the educational system of China.

Under the new regulations, the activities of schools of all types and grades, ranging from kindergarten to universities, have been carefully coordinated into one system.

The kindergarten, which had existed in China before 1949, was two years for kids from four to six years of age. Since then, it has been extended to three years, including children up to seven years of age, which is when they are admitted to the elementary school.

The Chinese term for nursery is *t'oh-erh-suo* (child trust institute), which means "the center where one entrusts his child to be looked after." The need for such institutions became obvious when parents who both worked outside the home had to leave their young children in someone else's care. There were a few nurseries in the cities of China before 1949, but it was only after the establishment of the People's Republic that nurseries flourished on a big scale and spread from urban to rural areas.

PHILOSOPHY

The three objectives of Chinese education are as follows: (1) To make education contribute to the ideological conversion of the Chinese people. The method employed is intensive Party control with intensified teaching of Party ideology. This is vividly illustrated in the songs mentioned in the introduction. Children not only sang songs in praise of Chairman Mao Tse Tung but also learned songs of hatred against all oppressors. Some activities included shaking fists and threatening to shoot down the planes of United States' imperialism and using wooden guns to bayonet caricatures of American generals and presidents. (2) To make education contribute to the national economy by using productive physical labor. This policy of instilling in all the love of labor is introduced at the preschool level. (3) To weave education into the life of the masses by developing education locally within local financial resources at all levels and standards to meet all local needs in accordance with local abilites.

Along with these objectives, the children are constantly reminded of the suffering and bitterness of prerevolutionary times. If children objected or complained about old and worn-out clothes, they were taught to be more appreciative by listening to stories of how bad conditions were in the old society. They are also told stories of heroes of the social reconstruction.

There is a great emphasis on team work, group action, or working together. Children are taught that friendship is more important than competition. For example, a group of children would work together on a painting. Some would paint in the background scenery, while others would do the grass or people in the foreground. They are made well aware of the fact that they are part of a production team.

Children are taken on field trips to factories and country areas. They are led to observe the poor and lower-middle class peasants working in the fields and notice the zeal and uncomplaining attitude of these folk. Consequently, children learn to focus their attention on society rather than on themselves.

Chinese Communist education makes the following assumption: corporate life is the foundation of socialism just as individualistic life is foundation of capitalism. Individualization must be destroyed to give way to socialization. Individualism, individual liberalism, individual heroism, and individual orientation are all terms of disrepute in Chinese Communist society.

Corporate living begins with the nurseries and kindergartens. Birthday parties, which are so popular in the kindergartens in Hong Kong, do not exist in the kindergartens in China because they are looked upon as occasions for the cultivation of individualism. Instead, people in China, young and old, come together to celebrate the birthdays of great social institutions, the anniversaries of the Chinese People's Republic, the Chinese Communist Party, the Chinese Liberation Army, etc.

Right from infancy, children are brought up feeling they are part of the great society and have their share in its assets and its well-being. They eventually feel that they belong to the public, the society, and the state more than they belong to their parents.

Nurseries and kindergartens have set clear goals. In addition to providing protective care while parents work, their purpose is to develop boys and girls who will continue the Revolution. Their program is planned to carry it out, and the Revolutionary Committee for a neighborhood area or a factory has the responsibility for seeing that objectives are accomplished and that the program is effective. Thus, there is a logical reason for the urgency to expand nurseries and kindergartens as fast as possible.

STRUCTURE AND EXTENT

Structure.

In the preschool stage, there is the nursery school for children from infancy to the age of four or five, which is followed by two to three years of kindergarten. Formal schooling starts at the age of seven in the primary school, finishing normally at the age of thirteen. As a main stream, students proceed to the regular or general secondary schools for six years of study.

Extent.

As is so often the case in present-day China, a conceptual change plays havoc with statistics. Data dealing with preschool facilities is a case in point; it must be split into two periods, pre- and post-1958.

Kindergartens and nurseries have never been widespread in China, and statistics on their development show that even as late as 1957, out of some 140 to 150 million children under seven years of age, there were only about one and a half million in formal establishments of this nature.

In general, the figures up to 1957 probably refer solely to urban child-care facilities built and operated by factories, mines, business enterprises, government offices, and city-block cooperatives. Their main function was to permit the mother to work, so that while some of these facilities were located in residential neighborhoods, many were maintained on the premises of the particular institution where the mother worked.

Even during this period of relatively slow growth, there were not enough qualified personnel to staff preschool institutions, and most of the teachers were housewives or young girls who had undergone very short training courses. Nevertheless, in the more progressive kindergartens there was an attempt to include such training as physical education, language, knowledge of social and natural environment, art, music, and number study.

In 1958, the reported number of children enrolled in "kindergartens" was almost thirtyfold over the preceding year, while the number in nurseries increased from half a million to over forty-seven million. Communist propaganda to the contrary, the figures for 1958 cannot be equated with those for 1957, and must be looked at independently. The growth coincides with the "leap forward," with the establishment of communes, and with the explicit policy of absorbing as many people as possible into the labor force. In the urban areas, more and more women entered plants and offices. In the rural areas, they were forced by the recruitment of millions of males into irrigation projects, road building, and the like, to perform a much greater share of agricultural labor. Whereas in the past, there had been some seasonal, informal accommodations to take care of children during the planting and harvesting seasons, the communes now provided year-round facilities for all children under school age.

The result is that the figures of 1958 and 1959 in no sense refer to what we would understand to be kindergartens. Although facilities for preschool child-care have expanded in the cities, the overwhelming increase is in the countryside where millions of children are watched over by illiterate or semiliterate old women or young girls while their mothers are working in the fields. They receive little, if any, instruction. Using averages, reported statistics indicated that there are about forty-five children in each group, supervised by two adults.

FINANCING

In the early 1970s in China, the government paid seven yuan a month for each child in kindergarten, while the parents paid four and a half or five yuan for a half year. They paid eight yuan per month for a half year for three meals per day for boarding preschoolers. In Tien Shan, the parents paid only five yuan (approximately $2.25 U.S.) per month for boarding pupils while the employee's factory welfare fund subsidized each child with another two yuan.

Because prices were very stable, the costs were very low for the people. Clothing and services for children were kept well within a price range all parents could afford.

ADMINISTRATION

Some preschools were run by local People's Councils while the majority were run by rural communes, urban factories, offices, industries, and residential areas. All of them had to be run according to regulations set out from time to time by the central Ministry of Education.

The revolutionary committees directed the provinces, the cities, the schools, the universities, the communes, the cultural groups and almost every other kind of organized activities in China. These committees are made up of workers or peasants in the country, leading bureaucrats, and people from the People's Liberation Army. The Ministry of Education controlled the location and facilities of each kindergarten as well as the qualification of the teachers and administrators.

FACILITIES

A woman's work load is lessened from eight to seven hours a day at the beginning of the seventh month of her pregnancy. Fifty-six days of maternity leave are granted to the mother, but this is flexible. It is extended if the birth has caused complications or if there are twins. The mother is allowed approximately half an hour off during the day to go and nurse the child in the nursery.

Naturally with a country the size of China, the situation would vary as far as early childhood education is concerned. Generally, the child would be left at home with grandmother. If there was no one in the home to care for the child and the mother was working in a factory, she would put the child in a factory nursery as early as eight weeks of age. She would simply bring the child to work, leave it in the nursery and then take it home after work. If the parents lived too far from a nursery to collect the child daily, boarding facilities would be provided so that they could leave the child during the week and collect him on Saturday afternoon for the weekend.

Some of the boarding institutions were converted old mansions—often the homes of dispossessed landlords. They consisted of a series of rooms around small courtyards and resembled the shared courtyard system of housing for the people seen in many large cities. In addition to attendants, cooks, nurses, and other ancilliaries, these institutions had one teacher for every seven or eight children who were three-and-a-half to five years old.

The buildings and equipment varied according to the wealth of the organization to which the institution belonged and according to the imagination of the teachers concerned. Sometimes the kindergartens were housed in their own buildings whereas at other times they occupied a few rooms in the primary schools. Classrooms varied in size from small rooms crowded with tiny desks, as in a building in Shanghai whose wooden floors and stairs appeared to be a considerable hazard, to a tall barn-like former landlord's house in a tea-growing village near Hangzhon, where the circle of children on tiny stools was dwarfed. Wherever possible, sleeping accommodations were provided for an after-dinner nap, or for more extended periods for the younger children. They slept on rows of matting-covered "kangs" (warmed brick platforms).

The furniture in these preschools is always carefully made to measure. The benches are just the right size, and a low basin and towel rack are provided. Some kindergartens had factory-made model animals, while others had tricycles for the children to play with.

TEACHER TRAINING

In 1956, the Ministry of Education estimated a need of over a million new teachers (on all levels) during the coming seven years. Against these figures, the total of graduates from the teacher training establishments was pitifully inadequate. An article in *China Reconstructs* for September 1956 noted that in 1955 twelve thousand new teachers had graduated, but the deficit in the schools was "at least 5,000."

Right up to 1961, there were not enough qualified personnel to staff preschool institutions. Most of the teachers were housewives or young girls who had undergone very short training courses. Nevertheless, in the more progressive kindergartens, there was an attempt to include such training as physical education, language, knowledge of social and natural environment, or music and number study.

Kindergarten teaching appeared to be exclusive to women since it was thought that women did a better job at this than men.

CURRICULUM

Although the main trend is toward day schools that are open for some eight to ten hours a day, some schools operate a half-day, four-hour system. As mentioned previously, some are boarding schools with the children going home only on weekends. In yet other cases, the kindergarten is a temporary affair, set up during such events as the harvest. Small fees are charged that help offset the cost of meals provided.

In these preschools, music is used as a channel through which to fulfill the requirements for the basic components in the program—morality, eduation, ideology, and labor, and, in their own words, "learning to love each." When the children put on performances at school, strong make-up including rouge, lipstick, and eyeliner is applied.

Productive labor is expected of everyone in China. As early as the kindergarten level, each child must spend one fifty-minute period each week sweeping floors, planting seeds, preparing vegetables for the meal, or being otherwise meaningfully occupied in productive labor.

Activities such as vigorous running and playing, calisthenics, and action games are included in each day's schedule.

Verbal skills in language are developed through conversation, storytelling, and singing. The general educational policy is to delay the teaching of written language until the child enters primary school. However, during their final year in kindergarten, the children are introduced to a few Chinese characters, mainly those used for popular political slogans. In some kindergartens the children are taught how to hold a pen correctly and make some basic strokes. The six-year-olds often memorize a few simple quotations from Chairman Mao. However, it must be remembered that one of the aims in the kindergarten is to provide full opportunities for development without undue pressure or strain on the children.

Rarely does one see pictures or toys depicting real or anthropomorphized animals or fairy-tale characters. The only pictures are those of Chairman Mao or social realism depictions of factory, commune, or revolutionary heroics.

At three years of age, many children attend these preschools where they spend their time painting, singing, dancing, and playing games. One school had a high wall around it and a slippery dip in the yard for the children.

A Daily Program. A closer look at the Ho Ping District kindergarten in Tienstin will afford an opportunity to see how some of these preschools operate. This school, which operates from 7 a.m. to 6 p.m., had eight classes and a staff of forty. The toys and games were very similar to those in other countries. There were miniature cars and soldiers made out of plasticine. The children put on a delightful performance with various musical instruments, some of them home-made.

There were games in which the children were blindfolded and then tried to replace a turnip made of felt on a felt board where the rabbit was waiting for his dinner. The game of fish, in which the child had to use a pole with string and hook attached to catch an origami fish in an artificial pool, required a great deal of concentration. Some of the children were sorting shells or marbles with chopsticks. This also demanded a great deal of dexterity. In one game, they formed a circle, and two of the children were blindfolded and given paper flowers to hold. They started from either end of the circle and were required to put the paper flower into one of the two flower pots in the center of the circle. The person who got the flower into the flowerpot first won the game.

The children generally have opportunities to visit factories and country areas. They usually visit the factories relevant to the work they are doing, which may be making paper bags for shoes or checking light bulbs. In this way, they are taught respect and admiration for work. People from the community are sometimes invited to visit the schools and talk to the children about the type of work they do.

Discipline. Hyperactivity and curiosity are discouraged gently and kindly. This discouragement is subtle and more effective, depending upon group support, group convergence, and group identity starting from three years old onward.

Children who misbehave are not treated with strict discipline. Instead, other children try to persuade the child to think of his shortcomings, and they persuade him to cooperate in general collectivism. When younger children leave school at the end of the day they walk home in a neat line, singing as they march, falling out at their homes as they come to them. According to the teachers, this keeps things orderly and eliminates mischief.

The teachers are also open to self-criticism and they encourage this so that they can improve themselves. The general approach is to correct mistakes if you have made any and guard against making any more. This goes back to the proverb, "Running water is never stale and door hinge is never wormeaten," which means, "The only way to avoid political dust and germs contaminating our minds is by our constant correction."

SUMMARY

Ever since the establishment of the People's Republic of China in 1949, there has been a sharp increase in the number of kindergartens and nurseries. Children are thoroughly indoctrinated in the concepts of serving the people. They are taught from all sides that the new society is much better than the old society.

At school, their curriculum includes physical education, language arts, and general knowledge. Physical education includes health habits, free play, gymnastics, and dance, while language arts include verbal skills, like conversation and storytelling.

The quality of education provided at the preschool level ranges from professionally conducted city kindergartens to the mere minding of children while their mothers go to work. In these schools, the care of children is based upon the three principles of "play, schooling and labor," the labor at this stage taking the form of looking after and cleaning furniture and equipment and feeding pets.

Chinese philosophy of early childhood education includes training the children to love the party leadership, the fatherland, socialism, people's communes, the people, labor, science, and public property. The Ministry of Education, under the direction of the government, heads the organization. This body is composed of workers from the rural communes and the urban communities.

Children attend nurseries only when there are not grandmothers or "aunts" at home to keep them. Most often though there are older people there who keep the Revolution fresh in the minds of the children both at home and at school. They come and tell stories to children even in the nurseries.

Teachers are trained in Chairman Mao's philosophy. All other psychologists are considered second to Mao. Anything that does not coincide with his philosophy is disregarded.

Facilities range from old mansions to parts of school buildings containing pictures of Chairman Mao and workers from the local districts. They have tricycles or building blocks but no fairytale characters or toys depicting real or anthropomorphized animals.

The children function in groups rather than as individuals in these institutions, some of which are boarding schools while others are only day care centers open for four to ten hours per day.

In 1949, China had a 20 percent literacy rate. It is now claimed to be between 80 and 90 percent. This is to a great degree the result of Mao encouraging peasants and factory workers to attend school. More than just the bourgeoisie are now being educated.

REFERENCES

Butler, Suzanne: *Impressions of China Today*. Paul Hamlyn Pty. Ltd., New South Wales, Australia, 1974.

Chen, T. Hsui-en: *The Marxist Educational Revolution*. Praeger Publishers, New York, 1974.

Collins, Ruth: *The Educational Digest*. September, 1977, pp. 57-58.

Elston, Wilbur: China Today, *The Detroit News*, November 3, 1972, pp. 25-27.

Endicott, Norman: *This Is China Today: A Fresh Look*. Friendship Press. New York, 1969.

Fraser, Stewart: *Chinese Communist Education*. Vanderbilt University Press, Nashville, Tennessee, 1965.

Goldman, R.J.: Early childhood education in the People's Republic of China, *Education Forum 41*, May 1977, pp. 455-463.

Hu, Chang-Tu: *Tradition and Change in Chinese Education*, 2nd edition. Teachers College Press, New York, 1974.

Jeffery, J.C. & Linderberg, L.: Visit to N.S. Kingdom in the People's Republic of China, *Childhood Education*, vol. 51, November, 1974, pp. 83-86.

Kennedy, P.: The Republic of China (Taiwan), *World Education Series*, 1977, p. 12.

Orleans, L.: *Professional Manpower and Education in Communist China*. Library of Congress, Washington, 1961.

Price, R.F.: *Education in Communist China*. Routledge and Kegan Paul, London, 1970.

Shangai Wen-Hui Pao. *Shanghai Wen-hui Daily*, June 20, 1959.

The Republic of China. China Publishing Co., Taiwan, 1972.

Tsang, Chiu-Sam: *Society, Schools, and Progress in China*. A. Wheaton & Co., Exeter, Great Britain, 1968.

World Survey of Education V. UNESCO, Paris, 1971, pp. 317, 318.

Chapter 6

EARLY CHILDHOOD EDUCATION
IN ENGLAND

MINETTE JEE

INTRODUCTION

CONCERN for the education of the young child in Britain is a long established tradition. It originally stemmed from social reform as a sort of rescue and relief operation. It has always been promoted with missionary fervor and even today priority is given to deprived children in areas of social need.

As a result of the Education Act passed in 1970, education has been compulsory for children from the age of five onwards. However, public provision of an education system for children under five is still only a recommendation, not a reality.

Historical roots have created very diverse attitudes to voluntary preschooling in its various forms and towards the infant school as the first stage in the compulsory system. The needs of the child determined the daily program in nursery schools, whereas the elementary school, the forerunner of the modern primary school, aimed at combatting illiteracy in the working class.

The decision that a child should start school at five years of age was made over a century ago, not as a result of contemporary research but in an attempt to ameliorate the wretched social conditions of child labor. Today, parents regard it as a privilege to send a child to a nursery school or class, and there is a high degree of parental cooperation. However, sending a child to an infant school is looked upon as a right or duty, and the parental pressure on a child in an infant school is quite different from the parental support given to one in a nursery school. Expectations that the child will learn the elements of literacy and numeracy in the first classes of the infant school create demands from parents to which children in nursery schools are not subject. Children in nursery schools are just expected to play.

The government's aim is that nursery education should be available within the next decade for children aged three and four whose parents request it. Meanwhile, priority will be given to disadvantaged children. It is anticipated that, for the majority of children, this will be part-time nursery education. Unfortunately, the existing provision for nursery education and day care is undeniably inadequate, even for priority needs.

ORGANIZATION AND ADMINISTRATION OF E.C.E. PROGRAMS

In Britain responsibility for children zero to five years is shared between the Department of Education and Science (D.E.S.) and the Department of Health and Social Security (D.H.S.S.), formerly the Ministry of Education and the Ministry of Health. Each department has traditionally provided different kinds of institutions. The Department of Education and Science administers nursery schools and classes for three- to five-year-old children, while the Department of Health and Social Security provides Day Nurseries for children zero to five years old, these being mainly custodial. The Day Nurseries meet the needs of children of working mothers, mothers who can't take care of their children, and those children whose home environment is not very healthy.

The responsibility for the control and direction of the statutory system of education in England lies in the hands of the Secretary of State for Education and Science, who must be a member of parliament and is an ex-officio senior minister of the Crown. The provision and maintenance of schools and the employment of teachers is delegated to the 104 Local Education Authorities (L.E.A.). Most County and District Councils are elected on party political grounds and the representatives on an education committee are not necessarily well versed in educational affairs, though professional advice is supplied by salaried officers.

The Chief Education Officer has no power in his own right, though some do exercise considerable influence. The control and direction of a primary school (a nursery school is part of primary education) is vested in the head teacher (principal). The English head teacher has more freedom and power than in any other country. This factor leads to the creation of superb schools where the head has vision and ability. However, where the head is weak and incompetent the schools deteriorate to a very low standard. The report of the Taylor Committee (1975) recommended that there should be more parent and community involvement in the management of primary schools.

The British System of Education is based on the Education Act of 1944 and the subsequent amendments of the principal act. The national policy is to provide a varied and comprehensive education service in every area.

Nursery schools may admit children from two years of age, though in actual fact, few enroll under three years. Primary schools may admit from the age of three years, but limited facilities and provisions cause the majority of children to start school at the beginning of the term before their fifth birthday. The maximum number of children allowed in a nursery class is thirty. The maximum number of children in an infant class is forty. In a nursery school, the adult/child ratio is 1:13, and every nursery school must be in the charge of a qualified teacher, even though at least half of the staff are qualified nursery nurses.

All nursery and infant classes are coeducational. There is no legal compulsion to send a child to nursery school. The Act states that children must receive an efficient full-time education that caters to the child's needs and abilities. Because very few parents educate their children at home, nursery schools have to fill this void.

The 1944 Act required Local Education Authorities to be sensitive to the need to provide nursery schools and classes for children under the age of five, but did not make the provision of nursery education obligatory. Hence, some L.E.A.s have made generous provisions and others none at all. Thre is a much larger number of nursery classes than nursery schools, the latter being a much more costly proposition. In fact, the English Nursery School, because of operating costs, has priced itself out of existence. Staffing is the most costly expenditure. In 1976, 45,000 children were in full-time and 100,000 in part-time preschool education. These totals represented just 10 percent of the children between the ages of two and five years. Only 600 nursery schools were in operation.

The system is financed in the main by money voted by Parliament from revenue raised through national taxation. Sixty-five percent of the cost is contributed by the government, which distributes these funds to the Local Education Authorities. This is supplemented by money voted by local authorities that they obtain from a local tax. Voluntary bodies are required by law to contribute to the capital expenditure on buildings provided by them. Statutory and Voluntary bodies share the responsibility for the provision and maintenance of schools, establishing a system of "dual control."

The Department of Education and Science does not intervene in matters of curriculum and teaching methods nor does it in any way control the content or the character of books supplied to schools. It does, however, seek to influence the quality of teaching and to raise standards through a body of Inspectors recruited from the teaching profession. They act in an advisory capacity, having a creative as well as an inspectorial function. Though they act as liaison officers between L.E.A.s and the D.E.S., they cannot give orders to L.E.A.s or to teachers.

A portion of the Inspector's time is spent conducting inservice training, and they frequently produce pamphlets with suggestions for teachers. They are regarded as a support service by the teaching profession and their impartiality is a great strength to the English system of education. Their prime task is to advise Her Majesty's Government, and, being appointed by the Crown, they are known as Her Majesty's Inspectors. In their unique position, they can see beyond the boundaries of the L.E.A.

L.E.A.s have their own inspectors and advisors who have a function quite different from the Inspectors mentioned before. They have an executive responsibility to advise on appointments, assist in the administration of the school system, and guide teachers in their work.

Teachers' salaries are fixed according to a national agreement, though they are not Civil Servants. Nursery and infant teachers are regarded as primary teachers and are paid, according to qualification, the same salaries as primary and secondary teachers. However, their career structure is limited in comparison with teachers of older pupils, which may be the reason why very few men are found in the ranks of nursery and infant teachers.

The practice of allowing the elected members of the Education Committee and groups of school managers to make appointments to headships and teaching posts is questioned by some members of the teaching profession. The advice and influence of professional officers in this regard varies from one L.E.A. to another.

Nursery nurses, who assist teachers in the nursery schools and nursery and infant classes, receive two years training at a college of Further Education with regular practical experience in local nurseries. There are no academic requirements for admission to the course. An N.N.E.B. certificate, instituted in 1945, is awarded to those who successfully complete both the theoretical and practical assignments.

The Government Think Tank (Central Policy Review Staff) recently recommended major expenditure for the development of services for young children with working mothers. They rejected the idea of setting up a single, cohesive service to meet all the needs of day care and nursery education for children under five and provide advisory and support services for parents. What they recommended was a reorganization of existing statutory and voluntary services to create some kind of order out of the present haphazard system. A much higher degree of coordination between day nurseries and nursery education needs to be established, rather than maintaining the existing divisions. Local authorities are urged to be flexible in their provisions, and a set of common standards is to be drawn up that all authorities would be expected to meet. It is also proposed that a unified policy group be set up outside the two departments traditionally involved in this area.

A few local authorities have provided on the experimental level multipurpose Preschool Centres administered by both departments catering to this age range. These centres have been developed along quite different lines, each designed to cater to the special needs of the area and seeking to bring together the best in the care and education of young children. These centres are being carefully monitored by the National Children's Bureau. They seek to provide a more flexible service than the conventional nursery schools and day care centers, and all are situated in areas of high social need.

All provide facilities for parents as well as children, and some combine the provisions of mother and toddler groups, play groups, and other informal classes as well as custodial care and nursery education. The staff consists of a qualified teacher, trained nursery nurses, and sometimes a social worker. In all centres, there is a close link with social and medical workers, yet these institutions tend to be isolated from the main stream of education.

Lack of adequate public provision has resulted in the formation of a number of nongovernmental organizations, such as the PreSchool Playgroups Association (P.P.A.), which receive government grants and also usually make a small charge to parents. These groups are organized by parents on a voluntary, part-time basis. In 1966, the D.E.S. gave a grant to the association to appoint a National Advisor. Since then both the D.E.S. and D.H.S.S. have increased their grants to provide more advisors and training and development officers. However, the P.P.A. remains essentially a voluntary organization.

Originally the P.P.A. was a forceful pressure group, advocating the expansion of nursery school provision by the Central government. Their policy changed in the 1970s, and they now claim that play-groups managed by parents are preferable to the nursery school or class, which forms part of the general system of education.

Because statutory nursery provision gives priority to areas of high social need, the play-group movement has spread rapidly in middle-class areas by organizations such as the "Save the Children Fund." One of their chief concerns is to support and encourage mothers in their demanding role. In 1977, this movement represented a million parents and their children and continues to grow. Eighteen percent of children under five attend playgroups, whilst 10 percent of the same groups attend nursery schools or classes.

Infant Schools

Up to this point, this paper has looked mainly at the organization and structure of nursery schools catering to children under five years of age. The organization of infant schools will now be discussed.

Infant schools in Britain accommodate children ranging in age from five to seven. The most exciting infant schools follow a system of family or vertical grouping. This is a nongraded grouping of five-, six-, and seven-year-olds. The idea behind this type of grouping is the premise that at these ages, language development is the most important learning. The theory is that in this type of grouping, the children learn from one another.

The five-year-old needs to talk to kids older than himself and the six- or seven-year-old can explain things to a five-year-old in plain, logical terms that are understood much easier than the terminology used by adults. This helps not only the younger child but also the older child who has practice using his verbal ability.

In horizontally grouped schools where children are all the same age, this interaction would not take place. Another advantage of vertical grouping is that with the range of learning being so wide the teacher has to work individually with the children. Above all, language development achieves a natural acceleration in this grouping.

Transitional family grouping, in which the seven-year-olds are separated from five- and six-year-olds, has been adopted in some schools. However, this grouping is not as desirable as complete family grouping. The younger child loses the example of the older child and is inhibited in his natural reach for higher levels. Furthermore, the seven-year-old is deprived of the chance to help others and loses the chance to exercise leadership qualities.

TYPES OF CURRICULUM AVAILABLE FOR E.C.E. PROGRAMS

The English nursery school or class has relied too heavily on spontaneous play on the part of the children and intuition on the part of the teacher. Indoor and outdoor play was guided by the teacher using a great variety of materials.

The present emphasis is to sensitize the teacher and nursery nurse to the way a child uses language and to develop his thinking skills so that his activities are based not only on his social and emotional needs but also lead to cognitive growth. His play should also supply a purpose for sustained effort, and there should be time for the teaching of specific skills. Though his activity is mainly self-chosen and the child is given considerable freedom to organize his own activity, intervention strategies are very carefully considered.

Each day things in the environment afford opportunities for enjoying variations of texture, shape, color, and sound, The nursery school deems it important to develop the child's personality towards self-reliance, independence, and cooperation. The aim is to lay the foundation for mathematics, science, and literacy with an emphasis on creativity. They do not go about trying to prepare the child for compulsory schooling. While the nursery school suffers from its isolation, the danger facing the nursery class is that it may become a downward extension of the school program.

No formal teaching is done in the nursery school or class. Stories, music, poetry, and nature are enjoyed in small informal groups. Children play at will, individually or in groups, whether it be indoors or out. Large toys and equipment for climbing are provided for energetic physical activities. Playing with water and sand provides opportunities for experimentation and a variety of materials leads to early scientific discoveries. Wood blocks and bricks are used for construction activity and clay, paint and crayons are available to help the child's artistic development.

Books, carefully chosen, stimulate the child's imagination and language, and literature plays an important part in the daily program. Dolls and appropriate furniture and equipment encourage social and domestic play. Some use is made of constructional toys and puzzles, but the emphasis is on experience and discovery as opposed to occupation with the child being encouraged to master his own environment.

Infant Schools

The infant school is concerned with the general development of children. The schools relate their approach to the current needs of the children and aim to provide full scope for their individual development.

In order to widen the children's experience, opportunities are provided for experimenting with materials such as sand, water, clay, paint, and wood. Kids build with bricks and boxes and participate in imaginative play, stories, and music. These activities are linked, where appropriate, with writing, reading, and simple arithmetic, the aim being to stimulate an interest in books as sources of information and pleasure, to introduce mathematical concepts, and to encourage fluency in oral and written expression.

Some infant schools have what is termed "the integrated day." The daily program includes creative, intellectual, artistic, and physical activities. Each student utilizes the school's offerings according to his own interests, abilities, and drives. The classroom thus becomes a workshop where students work individually or in small groups.

The integrated day introduces a different type of learning environment as children become excited about learning through discovery. When they are personally involved, they show a willingness to persevere with even difficult and tedious tasks.

The integrated day accommodates the natural flow of ideas, language development, and other learning experiences, thus making education a new kind of continuous progress. An endless variety of materials and apparatus is supplied and is easily accessible for all children.

Students make brief forays into different subjects in a short space of time with no time limit being set on these experiences. The child is thus exposed to many aspects of learning, sometimes being involved in deep concentration and at other times committed to less involved work or relaxation with one generally leading to another.

The teacher chooses the day's program, which the children integrate with their activities. However, the basic philosophy behind this program is one of "play." There is not much difference between work and play at this level and proponents allege that children don't see much difference between one subject and another.

When children report to school in the morning they find the day's planned activities listed on the chalkboard. Six children may start in the reading corner, six may start in the library alcove, and six may play at dressing up. Children are allowed to make choices and then follow through and work productively.

In continuation of the family grouping concept, there are no individual desks and children do not have assigned places. The rooms are equipped with a number of tables arranged in conjunction with bookcases to form a number of alcoves. The teacher does not have a desk and usually operates from one of the tables. She moves around continually, giving children individual help where needed.

Math. Infant schools approach mathematics through measuring, weighing, and graphs, e.g. a chart may be made illustrating the changeable weather over a period of time. By using charts and graphs, the child learns numbers, symbols, and shapes.

Children are given materials such as buttons, nails, etc. that they have to sort and classify, comparing sizes, shapes, texture, etc. Through this process they become familiar with the terms implying inequalities and other mathematical concepts.

Reading. Infant schools have been successful in the teaching of reading, evidenced by the fact that most five-year-olds can read. The methods used by teachers are wide ranging and include phonics and sight reading. The Initial Teaching Alphabet, developed by Sir James Pitman, is highly regarded by teachers and is used extensively.

Play. Most classrooms open onto an outside play area. This contains items such as rabbit hutches, tree logs, sandpits, climbing apparatus, and small gardens that the children work. The children use this area on an individual basis, i.e. they do not have to play with someone else. Set play times are not enforced, and frequently the children will stay inside the classroom all day.

Reward and Punishment. Corporal punishment still occurs, but the move is away from this type of punishment. The teacher should use other types of punishment, depending on the child's misbehavior. Praise and the satisfactory accomplishment of tasks are reward enough for most children.

PHYSICAL FACILITIES

Regulations concerning buildings and hygiene are standardized by the D.E.S. and D.H.S.S. One-story buildings are recommended with provision made for outdoor play and, where possible, space for gardens to be planted. A covered verandah leads to a sheltered and protected play court. Direct access to outdoor play from the indoor playrooms is essential, and flexibility is a feature of the newest buildings.

Recently, many nursery schools have been built on open-plan lines, but there are strong reservations as to whether this type of building is suitable for a centre providing both care and education. In recent years, they have been furnished in imitation of the home rather than in a mini-school fashion. The furniture is light, movable, comfortable, and cozy. Day nurseries tend to be far less clinical in appearance.

A room for parents is usually provided, though dual use of a staff lounge may be the solution to providing space for the many other adults in the community who will visit the unit. Parents are encouraged to visit the centres and to be actively involved in their child's well-being.

Furniture is designed less specifically for a particular purpose, and there is little distinction between the use of furniture and play with furniture. The predominance of the traditional children's chairs and tables has given way to more space-saving furniture including benches, worktops and screens, trolleys, and the use of a variety of textures and floorings including carpeting, tiling, linoleum, and cork. Furniture is not merely utilitarian but needs to be exploitable in ways by which children will discover possibilities unforeseen by the designer. Furniture that can be used casually and comfortably both by child and adult is recommended.

In infant schools, much of the above applies. As mentioned before, classrooms in these schools have tables instead of desks and these tables are arranged in such a way as to form alcoves for different activities. There is a math corner, a reading corner, an art corner, an area for play, and corners for other types of activities.

Work areas for messy activities are set up in the more uninviting alcoves. These nooks are usually located in corridors or cloakrooms. The children seldom notice their surrounding when engaged in this type of activity. Wide use is made of primitive materials such as water and sand.

There is a vast quantity of raw materials in every room. Most of this material is ingenious, inexpensive, and homemade. In addition to these raw materials, all of the infant schools have eye-catching displays such as a display of semiprecious stones, insects, stamps, and coins, with books on those subjects available next to the display.

All schools have collections of various kinds that are kept up to date and used daily. There may be such things as collections of strangely marked pebbles, differently shaped leaves, and a few special items that would make children think and compare. There is no limit to the types of materials that can be used in these schools.

The average nursery school has been established on the principle that "small is beautiful." Forty to sixty is the usual enrollment, though some authorities have built schools for 120 children. Most nursery schools have twenty children in a class.

An infant school or department has an average of six classes with 240 children on the roll. A few infant schools have auxiliary help that is mostly untrained for these teachers. Thus, a four-year-old in an infant school gets far less adult attention than in a nursery school or playgroup, and he is a part of a much larger community. If he is in an infant department, he may find himself on a playground with 500 other pupils.

Many teachers see this as an advantage because the head of the school knows the families attending and it makes for continuity. Nursery teachers claim this is a disadvantage as the infant class lacks the intimacy of a nursery school, and the inadequate parent does not easily form a good relationship with the teacher when numbers are large.

SUMMARY

Early childhood education in England is the responsibility of nursery schools or classes, which enroll children aged zero to five, and infant schools, which in their lower levels cater to children aged five to seven.

They fall under the jurisdiction of the Department of Education and Science and the Department of Health and Social Security. The Secretary of State for Education and Science is the individual responsible for the control and direction of the statutory system of education in England. The provision and maintenance of schools and the employment of teachers is delegated to Local Education Authorities.

Parliament provides 65 percent of the costs of schools with the rest being raised on the local level. No tuition fees are charged and books and materials are supplied by the state.

Nursery schools are in charge of a qualified head teacher, and in most cases, assistant teachers are also qualified. Each nursery class or group is staffed by the equivalent of a full-time nursery nurse as well as a teacher.

Infant schools, which fall under the primary school structure, have a head teacher, with qualified teachers in each classroom. The teachers don't have assistants.

In the nursery schools there are no formal lessons, but indoor and outdoor play is guided by the teacher using a great variety of materials. The intention is to develop the children physically and emotionally as well as educationally. Buildings and equipment are specially designed to meet the needs of small children.

The curriculum in infant schools focuses on language development, early scientific and mathematical ideas, physical coordination, and the development of social relationships and aesthetic responses. There is a more structured approach and direct teaching of the three R skills. Plenty of opportunities are also available for play activities.

Certain organizations, because of the lack of public provision, have established voluntary groups such as the Preschool Playgroups Association. They provide preschool services when the government cannot.

Whether serving in the first class of an infant school, in a nursery school or class, or one of the newly established Children's Centres, British teachers of young children will have to move into quite new territories of adult education and community development. Teachers, social workers, and nursery teachers will have to become managers and tutors of all the other adults who have a part to play in the early years of education. Above all, early childhood educators need to realize where their work fits into the whole process of education. They cannot remain in splendid isolation.

REFERENCES

D. Birchall: *Children's Centres*. National Children's Bureau, 1981.

Jerome Bruner: *Under Fire in Britain*. 1981.

Margaret Donaldson Fontana: *Children's Minds*. 1978.

Hughes, Mayall, Perry, Petrie, and Pinkerton: *Nurseries Now*. Pelican, 1980.

Chapter 7

EARLY CHILDHOOD EDUCATION IN THE UNITED STATES OF AMERICA

INTRODUCTION

CHILDREN are America's most important resource because they are our future. Their formative years are an important concern of the public and of public policy. Since World War I, children under six years of age have been spending more time away from their parents in a variety of situations. Approximately eleven million children under the age of fourteen are spending a substantial portion of their week in child care programs. Parents spent 6.3 billion dollars on child care in 1975.

The Federal Government, through the Department of Health, Education, and Welfare, provided approximately 2.5 billion dollars on additional child-care programs in 1976.

Child care is primarily the responsibility of parents. However, there are times when a parent has to be away from home, and on these occasions, it is important for parents to find the best care possible for their children. This care, unless an ably qualified baby sitter is available, is best found in a preschool education program.

The ideal is for the parent to be at home with the child during his formative years. When this is not possible, a suitable day care center is the next best thing. Above all, the child's welfare and development should be the primary consideration.

History of E.C.E.

Day care has existed in America for over 100 years, sponsored mainly by private groups. Government support and responsibility for day care quality is a recent innovation. The first day care centers catered to the poorer classes and started in the 1850s as social welfare institutions. These acted as temporary aids for working mothers until they were financially able to quit work and return home to care for their children (Cohen, 1978).

During World War I when mothers had to go to work in the factories, day care centers served as a temporary solution to the problem of child care. The intention was to disband these centers once the war ended. When World War II broke out, these children's programs obtained government funding for the purpose of freeing mothers to contribute to the war effort by going to work in factories, replacing the men who were with the armed forces.

Federal involvement in day care came in 1933 when day care was authorized as part of the Works Progress Administration. The idea was to create jobs for unemployed teachers, nurses, health and social workers, and related personnel. The popularity of this program suggested that there were widespread needs for such services. In 1942, the responsibility for these programs was shifted to the office of Defense, Health, and Welfare Services.

When the war ended, the day care system was disassembled, even though large numbers of women still remained in the work force. The number of women in the work force did decline during the late 1940s and early 1950s. However in the late 1950s and early 1960s, the trend began to change due to changing opportunities and basic economic considerations (Harris, 1979). More women started working outside the home and this trend has continued to rise since that time. The government had regarded day care centers as something of a temporary nature, but now it couldn't ignore the fact that it needed to be considered as a permanent institution (Cohen, 1978).

In recent years, there has been an upsurge in the use of day care. This is due to facts such as the increase in the number of women who have joined the work force, the rise in single parent families, and a new perception of the social roles of parents. Roby (1973) found that mothers worked because they had to—they were either divorced, widowed, separated, or their husbands were un-employed or earned incomes too low to support a family.

The percentage of women in the labor force has increased dramatically since 1955. The percentage for women with children six years or older has increased from 38 percent in 1955 to 58 percent in 1977. For women with children younger than six, it has increased from 18 percent to 41 percent (FIORC, 1978).

Single parent families number about 17 percent of the population today. In families where a female is the head, 58 percent of the mothers either work or are looking for work (FIORC, 1978).

Philosophy

The American philosophy of E.C.E. combines the theories of Piaget, Dewey, and those of the British Infant School. Piaget's theory of intellectual and moral development has been adopted as well as Dewey's philosophy regarding the child's own natural rhythms and maturational forces.

The British Infant School regards all children as active learners who can indicate to their teachers what their needs and wants are. Thus the daily program allows large blocks of time for the child to explore and investigate items of interest to him. Physical activities and movement occupy an important place in the program, and play and games are used to facilitate learning (Stevens, 1976).

Play figures prominently in the American philosophy. Play is a means of finding oneself, interacting with others, using symbolic thinking, and internalizing the norms of society. It is important for socioemotional and cognitive development.

Up until a few years ago, preschool programs were merely re-garded as babysitting services for the convenience of mothers. The teacher's role was that of a surrogate mother who performed all the tasks that the child's natural mother would perform. Anything else she did was to occupy and amuse the child and had no educational significance attached to it whatsoever. "In young children, activity, play, and learning are all of a piece. Indeed, quantity early education programs are predicated on this knowledge" (Elkind and Lyke, 1975).

According to Froebel, Montessori, and Pestalozzi, a child needs adult imposed structure in some domains and freedom from adult intervention in other domains. In the early years of life, the child needs structure in the social domain, imposed by adults, and freedom from intervention in the intellectual domain. The reverse is true when the child enters elementary school. "The kindergarten age is crucial in this regard and must provide the young child with a balance of freedom and structure in both the social and the academic domains" (Ibid). However, some modern theorists disagree with the notions that young children should be free from intervention in the intellectual domain, particularly in the case of children from impoverished economic backgrounds (Harris, 1979).

The care provided in day care centers should help the child better understand himself and his environment. Learning is encouraged as he plays with and shares in the experiences of peers and significant adults.

Objectives

The purpose of E.C.E. is to facilitate the progression of young children in social, emotional, cognitive, and motor development. Preschool programs work to increase the availability of developmentally appropriate activities. They also encourage adult/child interactions and provide ample opportunities for child/child interaction.

Many children suffer from nonstimulating environments, and day care programs seek to rectify this state of affairs. Children need experience with symbolization, and this skill is fostered by interaction with others. Children need to develop respect for self and others along with guidance towards impulse control. They need to be valued and feel important. The development of a positive self-concept is crucial to the mastery of the preceding skills and developmental areas.

Environments providing stimulation and appropriate early education experiences include the following: nursery schools, parent/child centers, home-based day care, Head Start programs, group care centers, home visitor parent training programs, at home with parents, relatives, or friends, and selected television viewing (Smith, 1978).

Let's consider some of the situations that have contributed to the proliferation of early childhood programs as delineated in the preceding paragraph. One situation that has had great impact is the absence of the mother from the home because of employment. During infancy and toddlerhood the chances are one in three; from ages three through school age the chances are one in two. A second situation is that children come from less than ideal home conditions. Children coming from poverty stricken homes number one in six; children from one parent homes number two in five; and children with adolescent mothers number one in five. Additionally, many children come from families who are experiencing stress, and two out of five of these children are not immunized prior to school age. Without participation in early childhood education programs, many handicapping conditions go undetected or undiagnosed until the child enters school (Ibid).

One can thus see why there is a need for assistance for these children during these early years. Preschool programs strive to meet this need. Centers have been established to provide care and valuable educational experiences and foster growth and development in all aspects of the child's life. Each child participates in activities that help him grow into a well-rounded individual who can interact effectively with those around him. The total development of the child is stressed.

ORGANIZATION AND ADMINISTRATION OF E.C.E. PROGRAMS

Prior to the 1960s, federal day care efforts were primarily a response to emergencies. In 1962, the Social Security Act was amended to authorize financial support for day care. Federal involvement was a response to a long-term social need. Day care centers were now designed to help working mothers and also to help individuals seeking to lift themselves out of poverty.

One of the mysteries of the American preschool system is the fact that twelve different agencies are involved in day care services. The responsibility for these services rests in agencies not primarily committed to the welfare of children. Elliot Richardson's statement in a policy research project report characterizes this dilemma in the following statement: "At the present time the Social Security Act, the Economic Opportunity Act, the Elementary and Secondary Education Act, and the Manpower Development and Training Act all contain child care or related provisions. Our intentions have been good and we have made some progress. But the scattered array of child care authorities has often led to confusion, duplication and waste" (Policy Research Project Report, Child Development Policy for Texas, No. 2, 1971). Under the provisions of Title XX funding, control of the federal program of day care services is vested in the Community Services Administration of HEW, instead of the Administration for Children, Youth, and Adults (1978).

1972 Proposed Federal Day Care Requirements (FDCR)

CARE SETTINGS. Applies to all federally supported day care, including in-home care, family day care, group day care homes and centers; contains specific requirements for each type of care.

AGE-SPECIFICITY. Recommends child-staff ratios according to age of child and type of day care; distinguishes among seven age groups for centers and three age groups for day care homes, recognizes the special needs of infants and toddlers. One caregiver is allowed to attend no more than three infants or four toddlers.

RATIO FOR CENTERS. One caregiver per 3 infants (0-1 1/2 yrs); per 4 toddlers (1 1/2-3 yrs); per 13 children (6-8 yrs); per 16 children (9-11 yrs); per 20 children (12-14 yrs).

RATIO FOR FAMILY DAY CARE. One caregiver per six children, provided at least half the group is over three; in no case may one adult care for more than three toddlers or two infants.

STAFF COMPETENCY. All caregivers required to possess specified competencies and be able to provide children with appropriate developmental activities according to a written plan or schedule; requires at least one staff member with specified educational or experience qualifications in each center serving 39 or more children.

ACCOUNTABILITY. Sets forth specific requirements to ensure accountability of day care operators; in providing programs that meet federal requirements; for supervision of staff; for keeping financial and other records; etc.

PARENT PARTICIPATION. Requires each facility serving 15 or more children to have a policy advisory council, consisting of 50 percent parents; requires administering agencies to evaluate and act upon complaints from policy advisory councils and parents in general.

In the administration of preschool programs, four areas need to be considered. They are planning, organization, supervision, and evaluation.

Planning involves the curriculum, daily schedule, equipment needed, and the activities in which the child will participate. The organizational aspect comes into play in the hiring and training of staff, setting up the daily program, and catering to the needs of children. Supervision takes place by observing the staff daily to make sure that the planned program is implemented. Teacher performance, child behavior, and the effectiveness of the learning environment are evaluated regularly.

Each day care center has a board of directors consisting of a chairman, executive secretary, and a finance committee. The size of the program determines the number of people serving on the board.

The chairman, who serves for one year, convenes meetings, is an ex-officio member of the various board committees, and helps foster the objectives of the day care center. The executive secretary is the actual director of the program. He serves on the executive committee and prepares the agenda for board meetings. The executive and finance committees prepare the budget and also provide financial reports for each board member.

The board determines the needs of the center and monitors expenditures as authorized in the budget. The board also hires and employs the center's director, determines employment policies, and sets guidelines for eligibility of enrollment and attendance.

The board of directors has a responsibility towards the community it serves, the staff of the center, and the children which the program serves.

Insurance policies are taken out to cover fires, liability, accidents, and workmen's compensation. Auto insurance is also necessary when the center has its own transportation service.

Types of Day Care

Day care programs are divided into three main groups: In-home care, family day care, and center care. Although the organization of day care programs may take many different forms, most of them fit into one of these three categories.

In-home Care (37%). About 2.6 million families use in-home care ten or more hours per week (Unco, National Childcare Consumer Study, 1975).

Advantages: Child is in a familiar place; hours scheduled to fit routine of family; the caregiver performs more than one function (cleaning, cooking, etc.) as well as being responsible for the child; and the child can learn practical lessons, such as home upkeep.

Disadvantages: This type of care can be expensive: 5,000 dollars per year or more for full-time care if the caregiver is paid the minimum wage required by law. There are also wide differences in the type of care provided. Peer interaction and exposure to a variety of situations is not a highlight of this program.

Family Day Care (47%). Approximately 3.4 million families use this form of care ten or more hours per week (Unco, National Childcare Consumer Study, 1975).

Advantages: Flexible hours and convenient locations; a variety of ages are accommodated; the child interacts with other children, and parents can choose a caregiver who shares similar views on child rearing and development.

Disadvantages: Some of these programs are unstable, the caregiver frequently shutting down operations; there is seldom professional assistance to ensure the adequacy of the care offered. The parent has no way of knowing whether the provider has the proper qualifications for the job.

Center Care (16%). Nearly 1.3 million families use this form of care ten or more hours per week (Unco, National Childcare Consumer Study, 1975).

Advantages: Predictable hours of operation; a stable location; a wide variety of group interaction and learning experiences; a licensed program; and professional staff.

Disadvantages: Fixed hours at the center may not correspond with the parents' work schedule; the location may be inconvenient; lack of a home atmosphere; the danger of regimentation in child rearing methods; and the possibility that parents may not be able to choose a caregiver with similar goals for childrearing.

The figures and percentages given for the three categories do not include those children who benefit from day care less than ten hours per week. These figures were also based on the 1975 National Childcare Consumer Study.

According to more recent figures, most youngsters are cared for in their own homes or in the homes of relatives (61%). The next largest group is in family day care programs (31%), with the remainder being cared for in centers (8%) (Prescott, 1978).

The programs in centers consist of two types: Closed structure, where the teacher makes most of the decisions, and open structure, where the children initiate activities. In the closed structure, children's activity segments are initiated and terminated by adults 58 percent of the time. The percentage of adult decisions in the open structure is 20 percent, 13 percent in family day care, and 7 percent in home care programs.

In a closed structure, structured activities such as toileting, waiting for lunch, etc. occupy 24 percent of the child's time, whereas in an open structure the percentage drops to 10 percent and is even lower in home-based programs—3 percent (Prescott, 1978).

Preschool Programming

The various forms of preschool programming will now be discussed.

Family Child Care. This program takes place in a private home. They are required to be licensed by the Welfare Department and care for up to six children under sixteen years of age, including those in the host family.

Home Play Groups. Three or four mothers organize this program with similar aged children. They meet in the morning or in the afternoon and rotate homes either daily or weekly. The host mother serves as the teacher and plans as well as initiates learning activities, while the other mothers enjoy a few hours of free time. Although the places change, the schedule of activities is usually the same. It includes indoor and outdoor play, story-telling, music, and other similar activities.

Parent and Child Teacher Program (PACAT). This is primarily a home-based program where parents are responsible for the child's learning. A trained teacher directs the parents in their planning and administering the program. Parents and children visit the school once a week, when the teacher gives special instructions to the parents and the children are allowed to work with classroom materials. Monthly parent-teacher seminars are held for the purpose of providing inservice training for the parents as teachers (Kuzma, 1978).

Family Day Care. These are run by day care mothers who have a knowledge of child development, nutrition, are able to plan and run a program, and can establish relationships with the parents. They are funded by Title IV-A funds (Sulby and Diodati, 1975).

Child Care Aide Service. This service is offered by some churches whose responsibility is that of referral. Individuals needing someone to take care of their child can contact the church who will then fill the position with a trained child care aide. The aide is paid by the person requesting the service (Kuzma, 1978).

Parent Cooperative Child Care Program. These programs are owned and operated by the parents whose children participate in them. The programs run for part of the day and serve parents who don't have to work a full day. Some full-day programs have been established on college campuses where a varied number of hours of child care service per day is needed.

Head Start. This is a preschool program for economically disadvantaged youngsters. These programs are federally operated and try to compensate for the child's deprived background. It caters to children aged three to five.

This program was started in the 1960s and has been one of the most innovative programs ever mounted on behalf of America's children. It is aimed at providing educational, social, psychological, health, and nutritional services to economically disadvantaged children. This program has been run at a cost of over 400 million dollars per year and has attempted to enrich the lives of these children by offering a broad spectrum of social services.

Since its inception, Head Start has suffered many hardships and disappointments. Many educators have pronounced it a failure and a waste of taxpayers' money. However, the parents of children who attend these programs praise and support them. Arguments against Head Start include the belief that the effects of Head Start fade after a year or two in elementary school. Other arguments show that Head Start has long-term effects (Zigler, 1978).

Lazar and others (1977) reported the findings of fourteen longitudinal studies of low-income children who participated in experimental infant and preschool programs over the past decade and a half. They list the following conclusions:

1. Infant and preschool services improved the ability of low-income children to meet the minimal requirements of the schools they enter. This effect can be manifested in either a reduced probability of being assigned to special education classes or a reduced probability of being held back in grade. Either reduction constitutes a substantial cost reduction for the school system.
2. Low-income adolescents who received early education rate their competence in school higher than comparable adolescents who did not have preschool education.
3. As measured by the Stanford-Benet and the WISC tests preschool programs produce a significant increase in the intellectual functioning of low-income children at least during the critical years of primary grades in schools.

Long-term effects depend on two simple factors: parents should be involved in the education of their children at home and schools should follow the Head Start program with further intervention efforts. There needs to be a continuity of purpose and developmental goals from home to Head Start, through kindergarten to primary school.

Despite criticisms and arguments against its usefulness, it appears that Head Start is here to stay.

Brookline Early Education Project

This is a preschool program that bears mentioning. Started in 1973, it serves more than 250 children and their families. This project operates as part of the Brookline, Massachusetts public school system and provides parents with help in their role as the primary teachers of their preschool children. The BEEP regards parents as the most important teachers in a child's life.

At the BEEP, complete physical and psychological tests and checkups are given regularly at no cost. The family pediatrician is closely involved if any problems are detected.

Teachers visit the homes regularly, and after the age of two, the child attends a regular playgroup session at the BEEP center. A prekindergarten program is available at the age of three for a nominal fee. In these instances, children and teachers meet three or four times per week. All other services, besides prekindergarten, are free. These include transportation to and from the center, a library, and other facilities. The major portion of funding comes from the Carnegie Corporation of New York and the Robert Wood Johnson Foundation (Whitesides, 1977).

Financing of Programs

Some programs are completely funded by tuition fees. Others receive funds from Community Chest, United Givers Fund, or individual contributions. Community support helps families who otherwise could not afford the services offered.

Federal funds are also available for day care programs. In these cases, the program must follow local, state, and federal day care regulations. Requirements can be obtained from the Department of Health, Education, and Welfare.

Day care centers run for the benefit of employees of institutions or businesses are subsidized by those institutions. This aid may be in the form of money, equipment, or food. Programs run by church groups often have the free use of church facilities, janitorial, and maintenance services.

Private nursery schools and kindergartens are patronized by people who are well off and their fees are large enough to completely support the programs. Child Care Centers are funded by the state and by fees charged on a graduating scale according to family income and the number of children in school. Head Start is funded by the office of Child Development of HEW, and Project Follow Through and Title I funds are administered by the U.S. Office of Education.

Other support is obtained through special fund raising campaigns, small business loans, and free services provided by certain agencies.

E.C.E. CURRICULUM

Although the choice of curriculum is an individual thing, there are some basic areas that are essential to all E.C.E. programs. They are basic because almost all of the educational objectives of a day care center can be met through them. These areas are the library, art, housekeeping, blocks, and puzzle and table games.

Activities in these areas touch on the physical, emotional, and intellectual needs of adequate growth and development. Also, kids don't mind being involved in these activities daily. These span the full range of sophistication, supervision, and group size. They can also be used in both free play and structured activities. The curriculum should not be limited to these areas, but they should not be excluded, regardless of what else is included. Within these areas, flexibility should be a primary objective.

Library

The emphasis in this area is on language development, stories, books, quiet play, and the general enjoyment of literature. It should be spacious enough so that children can be accommodated comfortably to hear a story. The reading of stories or the location of books shouldn't be limited to the library, however.

Art Area

This area is the most diverse of the five basic areas. Activities engaged in in this area include drawing, painting, cutting, pasting, clay, and papier-mache modeling. More than one activity could be in progress at one time, or a single activity may be popular enough to involve all the children.

Exposure to a variety of media is emphasized. Children should feel free to just dabble and experiment with art materials. They should also receive instructions in the use of materials.

Art activities provide an outlet for fear, hostility, and tension and also encourage nonverbal communication. The children are encouraged to use their imaginations, although adult guidance is sometimes needed. The teacher should create an atmosphere that encourages free expression. Children will comment about their own drawings and paintings and thus reveal their needs and emotions.

Art can initiate other activities or can be a byproduct of other activities. It can be integrated into most activities, e.g. decorating a room for a party, painting carpentry projects, construction of puzzles, etc. (Evans, 1971). In order for art to be effective, it shouldn't be overused.

Housekeeping Area

This area, no matter what the ages of the children are, is both a source of security and a catalyst for role-play. Children learn societal roles, and they can explore and act out roles of people they see. They learn to understand the rules of society and the reasons behind the way it functions. Other areas also elicit dramatic play, but this area is the only one guaranteed to bring forth such a response. By watching the children closely when they are busy in this area, the teacher can learn a lot about each one of them.

The areas represented here are usually the kitchen and the bedroom. They are readily identified with by children and are the easiest to set up (Evans, 1971).

Block Area

Preschool classrooms everywhere almost always have a block area. Most elements of the preschool curriculum can be initiated from this area. For example, dramatic play in this area rivals that of the housekeeping area. Children can build boats, planes, stores, etc.

This area provides the means for introducing number concepts. For example, you could ask a child how many four inch blocks would be needed to make a twelve inch block. These questions can be visualized in the context of an interesting activity, and the concept is formed as a natural consequence of that activity.

Other benefits coming from this area include articulation of ideas and learning the vocabulary of size and shape.

Puzzles and Table Games

This area is one of the most difficult to set up. However, children can work here without much supervision, and it results in a very productive educational experience. Areas that are introduced and can be learned from such activities include language development, observation skills, individual concentration, number concepts, and abstract reasoning (Evans, 1971).

In addition to the five basic areas discussed so far, other areas should be added that are also important in the preschool classroom. They do not require a permanent place in the room, and their activities can be incorporated into the five basic areas.

Water Play

All kids love to play with water, to splash, pour, and make bubbles. However, water can teach children the sense of floating and sinking, solubility and insolubility, weight, volume, colors, and optics.

Language skills develop as children talk about what they are doing. Water is also a springboard for a social studies activity.

Sand Play

This type of play is just as versatile as water and serves as a good teaching device. Wet and dry sand are equally effective and most children find satisfaction in using them.

Carpentry Area

Although many people may regard this area as being too dangerous for children, danger can be avoided by using adult tools and not children's tools and stressing that these are not toys, but tools that should be treated with respect. A limit on the number of children in this area and the provision of adult supervision at all times will ensure that the children are not in danger; they'll thus learn to use tools safely.

Children don't have to produce something elaborate. Sawing a board in half or nailing two boards together is productive in itself. Simple toys can be created, but all creations should be equally important. When something has been constructed, the children can move into the art area and paint their product.

Carpentry affords the child a feeling of accomplishment as he constructs something functional from scratch. Other benefits of this program are the development of small-muscle control, eye-hand coordination, and an awareness of the physical capabilities of an individual (Evans, 1971).

Large-Muscle Activity

This is usually accomplished outdoors, but it should be provided for indoors, in case of foul weather outside. Sometimes the teacher does not have time to take the children outdoors, yet their large muscles need to be exercised. This activity area depends on the amount of space available.

Music

Rhythm and movement are a natural part of a child's makeup. Singing and other musical activities encourage self-expression in a number of ways.

Language, Numbers, and Social Studies

These areas are so much a part of the total curriculum that it is not necessary to set aside a fixed area for them. For example, if a child has a birthday party, the cutting of the cake can be used as an opportunity for teaching fractions. The eating of a watermelon can be used to teach size and weight comparison, and as for the social studies aspect, the class could discuss where the fruit came from, how it travelled from the farm to the school table, etc. The descriptive vocabulary and conversation are excellent for the development of language skills. All these skills can be taught, capitalizing on the various opportunities offered by the daily schedule (Evans, 1971).

Outdoor Play Area

This area provides opportunities for the child to explore, experiment, learn, and exercise. The child also learns to be creative, develop language skills, and interact with his peers.

FACILITIES AND MATERIALS

When considering facilities for a preschool program, one needs to consider the aims, objectives, and purposes of the program in determining how many people will be accommodated. The size of the facility is very important.

Classrooms are arranged so that children can move about easily and choose the activity in which they want to be involved. There are areas for block building, a household center for imaginary play, a corner for records, books, rhythm instruments, facilities for painting, clay modeling, water and sand play, and other kinds of sensory experiences.

The choice of equipment and toys should take into consideration the developmental level of the children. They should challenge the child to learn and broaden his interests and skills.

The materials and facilities used will be listed under the broad curriculum areas discussed in the previous section.

Library: shelves, seats, books, pictures, plants.

Art: paint, brushes, paper (all types), easels, clay, crayons, chalk, glue, chalkboard, pipe cleaners, magic markers, paper cutter, stationery, scissors, yarn, string and twine, wire.

Housekeeping: dolls, mirrors, dress-up clothes, household furniture (child size), for the kitchen and bedroom areas.

Blocks: unit blocks—hollow blocks, table blocks, cardboard blocks, Jumbo Lego® Bricks.

Puzzles and Table Games: puzzles (large pieces and bright colors), pegboards, giant blocks in all sizes, shapes and colors, construction sets, lotto, beads, empty thread spools, abacus, table blocks.

Water Play: buckets, coats, strainers, funnels, tin cans, straws, soap suds, sponges, boats, tubing, etc.

Sand Play: cups, scoops, spoons, funnels, strainers, etc. Uses same materials as those used in water play.

Carpentry Area: worktable, hammer, nails, saw, ruler, hand drills, sandpaper, T-square, screwdriver.

Large-muscle Activity: balls, punching bag, tumbling mats, hula hoops, bicycles, slides, climbing structures, swings, wagons to pull or push, rocking boat, seesaws.

Music: record player, piano, rhythm instruments, bottles, bells, records, etc.

Language: pictures, posters, photographs, picture lotto, books, typewriters, etc.

Numbers: materials from other areas are used, e.g. puzzles, blocks, water, sand, dominoes, all help to develop number concepts.

Social Studies: maps, globes, dolls, musical instruments, field trips. This area should be thoroughly integrated into the total classroom activity.

Outdoors: sand, dirt, water, wheeled vehicles, building materials, climbing structures (Evans, 1971).

Children could also take care of pets such as fish, gerbils, mice, insects, turtles, dogs, and cats. They can develop a sense of responsibility in caring for them.

Meals

Children are fed two, sometimes three meals a day, depending on how much time they spend at the center.

Teacher Training

Teachers should have a four year degree in Early Childhood Education or a two year degree in Child Development. Subject areas include behavioral sciences, fine arts, social sciences, language, literature, philosophy, mathematics, physical and biological sciences (Leeper, 1968). Teachers have either state or church certification, a Child Development Associate credential, or a Child Center Permit.

Periodic seminars, workshops, and refresher courses are necessary so that the teacher can keep abreast of developments in child care research. These should enable the teacher to improve her teaching skills and to make appropriate adjustments to the program.

SUMMARY

This chapter has attempted to give the reader an insight into the system of preschool education in this country.

Day care centers first served as a social tool and were regarded as a temporary service during the war years in order to allow women to work in factories releasing men for duty in the war effort. With a large number of women working in this day and age, day care centers have become a necessary part of our society.

Preschool programs consist of three basic types: in-home care, family day care, and center care. They all aim to facilitate the social, emotional, cognitive, and motor development of the child. Without proper motivation and guidance, the total development of the child will not be accomplished.

Funding for day care programs is provided by federal, state, and local authorities as well as by private groups, individuals, and parents. Certain regulations have to be followed by those receiving government support.

The curriculum offered in these programs varies. This depends on the type, size, location, and objectives of the program. However, most offer activities including music, reading, sand and water play, block building, games, and housekeeping areas.

The facilities vary according to the individual program. Teaching materials are based on the curriculum content.

Teachers usually have attended a four year or a two year college program relevant to early childhood education. Whatever their educational background, all have one objective—the total development of the children in their care.

REFERENCES

Cohen, Donald and Zigler, Edward: Federal day care standards, *Young Children*, March, 1978, pp. 24-31.

Elkind, David and Lyke, Nancy: Competition or cooperation, *Young Children*, September, 1975, pp. 393-399.

Evans, E., Shub, Beth, and Weinstein, Marlene: *Day Care*. Boston, Beacon Press, 1971.

Harris, S.T.: A Study of Colorado Policy Makers' Attitudes and Perceptions About Selected Issues in Prekindergarten Education. Doctoral Dissertation, University of Denver, 1979.

Host, Malcolm: *Day Care Administration*. Washington, D.C., Office of Child Development, 1971.

Kuzma, Kay: *Guidelines for Child Care Centers*. Washington, D.C., General Conference of Seventh-day Adventists Office of Education, 1978.

Lazar, I. et al.: *The Persistence of Preschool Effects*. Final Report to the Administration on Children, Youth and Families, Office of Human Development Services, U.S. Department of Health, Education and Welfare. October, 1977.

Leeper, Sarah: *Good Schools for Young Children*. New York, MacMillan Company, 1968.

Policy Research Project Report: *Child Development Policy for Texas, No. 2*. Austin, Texas, Lyndon B. Johnson School of Public Affairs, University of Texas, 1971.

Prescott, Elizabeth: Is day care as good as a good home? *Young Children*, January, 1978, pp. 13-19.

Roby, P. (ed.): *Child Care—Who Cares?* New York, Basic Books, Inc., 1975.

Smith, Marilyn: How could early childhood education affect families?, *Young Children*, September, 1978, pp. 6-13.

Stevens, Joseph: *Administration of Early Childhood Education Programs*. Toronto, Little, Brown and Company, 1976.

Sulby, Arnold and Diodati, Anthony: Family day care: No longer day care's neglected child, *Young Children*, May, 1975, pp. 239-247.

Whitesides, Barbara: The Brookline Early Education Project, *Young Children*, November, 1977, pp. 64-68.

Zigler, Edward: America's Head Start Program: An agenda for its second decade, *Young Children*, July, 1978, pp. 4-11.

Chapter 8

EARLY CHILDHOOD EDUCATION IN MEXICO

LILLIAN M. LOGAN

INTRODUCTION

IN order to understand the contemporary scene in the education of young children in Mexico, it is important to note the
interplay of foreign and indigenous forces that have brought about
the present configuration.

From an educational program organized sequentially and cu-
mulatively around the theories of Froebel, Montessori, Larroya,
Decroly, Dewey, Pikevitch, and Piaget, a concerted effort was
made to establish a purely Mexican *Jardin de Niños* (kindergarten). The struggle to develop an indigenous, nationalized, socialized, and vitalized institution took the efforts and total commitment of such leaders as Rosaura Zapata, Estefania Castaneda,
Lenor Orellano Lopez, and Bertha Von Glumer, reaching fruition
largely through the combined efforts of Señorita Beatrice Ordenez
Acuna, currently Director General of the Department of Preschool
Education, and Dr. Laura Rotter, Director of the Laboratory of
Psychological and Pedagogical Research, a branch of the Department of Preschool Education under the Ministry of Education in
the Federal District of Mexico.

History

The roots of the Mexican kindergarten were tentatively established in 1904. Not until 1928, however, did the Ministry of Edu-

cation move to unify the program for young children in both urban and rural areas.

Throughout its history, the Mexican educational system, beginning with the preschool level, has been influenced by the political situation existing in the republic. Ministries and governments came and went, but Señorita Rosaura Zapata, chief of preschool education for over fifty years, brought stability and continuity to the program by her concern for the development of an indigenous kindergarten with emphasis on the child and his growth in the Mexican milieu.

Soviet influence. Problems arose, however, during the 1930s when the kindergarten came under the influence of Soviet educational theory causing the Mexican cultural aspects of education to temporarily shift its orientation.

Among the conspicuously non-Mexican features of this period were

1. an emphasis on the proletarian child as the worthy recipient of educational opportunities;
2. stress on rational perceptions of the environment and phenomena;
3. the establishment of annexes to the kindergarten wherein younger children were cared for while their mothers worked;
4. the enlistment of parents, teachers, and children as active agents for social change;
5. an emphasis on physical health in the young child's development; and
6. a focus on activities that indoctrinate in the child a love for the worker and one's country. Children, especially in the rural kindergartens, were early initiated into the practices of collectivistic habits and group cooperative enterprises.

Criticism of the non-Mexican theoretical and philosphical approach to kindergarten education was centered not alone on the type of activities, but on the fact that the kindergartens were removed from the Department of Education and placed under the Department of Public Welfare.

Rosaura Zapata, chief of preschool education stated, " . . . During this period from 1934 to 1940 . . . the authorities were not interested in the intellectual development of the young child. Their objective was physical development for the child and emancipation of the mother with the resultant emphasis on custodial care for the young child . . . . "

Another point of contention was the annexation of the first two years of primary school to the kindergarten complex, which was in direct conflict with the theories of education in Mexican kindergartens at that time.

Perhaps the greatest area of conflict was the chasm between the Soviet emphasis on the scientific materialistic explanation of life as contrasted with the Mexican emphasis on the home as the center of social life and the community as the focus of the expression of love for one's country.

Fortunately, the dominance of Soviet educational theories, philosophies and instructional procedures was abruptly terminated when the succeeding ministry came into power. Preschool education was moved back under the auspices of the Ministry of Education—a move welcomed by leaders, teachers, parents, and children.

Thus in the fifties, early childhood education in Mexico once again began to emphasize the needs of the child in a social environment.

Philosophy and Objectives

The highly centralized system of education in Mexico has sought to combine activity and methods with political indoctrination, making use of the local environment as the focal point from which learning experiences radiate until regional, national, and ultimately international culture is absorbed and understood.

Art, music, literature, love for one's family and the community, and the expression of appreciation were the main objectives in the Mexican view of the young child. The child was given experiences in a healthful environment in which optimum intellectual, physical, social, and emotional development could be attained through the medium of games, music, dance, and dramatization in an outdoor environment and through excursions into the neighborhood.

In Mexico in the 1950s, emphasis was placed on organization of the learning environment to effect certain desired responses in a primarily group-oriented setting in which as many as 900 children were enrolled in a particular kindergarten. Today, however, the emphasis is on providing the individual child with educational experiences which stress interaction with the environment and development of skills that enable him/her to achieve his/her maximum potential and control and modify his/her environment. In other words, the development of the individual is a corollary to contributing to the society in which he/she lives.

closing   As the population explosion in Mexico continues, so does the concern for the education of the multitudes. Education for survival is not enough; education for leadership and followership, for cooperation and interdependence, for coping and succeeding in a world in which decisions must be made by a literate society are challenges that must be met.

There is currently a deep commitment to the development of every child to the maximum potential—the handicapped as well the gifted; the slow learner as well as the overachiever. This concern is well expressed by Dr. Rotter, director of the Research Laboratory: "We are looking at the development of each child; we are using scientific methods for diagnosing, analyzing, planning and prescribing, and keeping records of the success of our prognosis. Each teacher has a part in planning a program for the children in her group which meets individual needs for coping with the society in which he finds himself. This entails looking at and taking into account the cognitive, psychomotor, affective and creative needs of the child. It implies creating an environment in which the child has opportunity to communicate, experiment, create, and to discover his world and learn to solve problems which are significant to him at his particular stage in life."

ORGANIZATION AND ADMINISTRATION

Administration

The highly centralized national system of education in Mexico, in which the kindergarten is the first step in the educational ladder, has always played a dual role: that of an educational agency and of a socializing vehicle in the community.

The office of General Direction of Preschool Education remains today as the central agency responsible to the Minister of

Education in Mexico for the education of children from ages three through six. At the completion of the three-year kindergarten, children are ready to enroll in the primary schools of the various states of Mexico as well as in the capital city, Mexico, D.F.

The federal government in Mexico, D.F., is responsible for the administration of the program for all children—the normal as well as the special ones living in the federal district. The states are responsible for educating children within their jurisdiction. However, the federal government is a coordinating agency and on invitation provides consultation and advisory services to the states on terms of priorities for the services requested.

Currently, emphasis is on providing the states with leadership from the central government and on supplying suggested curriculum guides, the development of which teachers have been involved in.

The federal government is also responsible for setting the length of the school year in order to facilitate educational mobility within the country. All children in Mexico now have the same length of school year, from September through June, regardless of the area in which they live. Formerly, the school year was based on climactic considerations, thus varying the times schools were opened.

Funding and Tuition

Federal and state funding is available on the basis of economic needs of the district. For example, responsibility for providing the physical plant is assumed by the government. The kindergarten is established at a site in an area where there is opportunity for outdoor activities and play. The equipment, however, in all kindergartens is the responsibility of the parents in the school district. In affluent areas, parents readily pay for the needed equipment. In areas of low income, parents form organizations and make much of the needed equipment, contributing supplies that are essential. In such areas, teachers have a lot of "missionary zeal" and commitment and so contribute a sizeable amount of materials for the children to use.

Parents wishing to have a school established in their community present their case to the Department of Preschool Education and are given a hearing by the authorities. Tuition that is required from parents of all kindergarten children is determined on the socio-economic level of the district in which the school is established. The policy of charging a fee for kindergarten education is based on the belief that parents have a sense of pride in sending their children to kindergarten even if it means a sacrifice, and since compulsory attendance at school is not required until the child is seven years of age, it is felt that no one is discriminated against because of poverty. Parents have been known to collect a purse for a child when its parents have been unable to pay the tuition. Teachers, too, frequently dip into their pockets to "help out."

Extent

In 1904, there was only one kindergarten director, but by 1978 there were 1,000, looking after the preschools, of which 900 were situated in Mexico City. There were 160 inspectors for these schools, and eighty for the remaining states of Mexico. However, the responsibility of the inspectors in Mexico City extends throughout the states of Mexico, and they are frequently called upon as curriculum consultants, speakers for various conferences, and as representatives for the government at world organizations for early childhood education.

At the present time, there are fewer kindergartens established in the affluent areas. Many children whose parents can afford it are sent to private schools thus taking the strain off the public purse and making it possible for more kindergartens to be established in the less affluent districts.

Teacher Training

In Mexico, the kindergarten teachers have always been an elite class with higher academic qualifications—an extra year of education at the university and specific personal qualities.

Private schools for young children are also under the supervision of the Department of Education and must meet the standard set for government schools, both as to curriculum guides and in the qualifications of teachers. In order to teach in a kindergarten, one must have a four-year degree following secondary education plus an upgrading policy that requires work in a specialized area such as music, art, drama, puppetry, and special education. To be in line for the position of director of a kindergarten, the teacher must have had at least ten years of successful teaching, five years of training, with a specialization; also a competitive examination that includes competencies, theory, and personal qualifications must be taken.

Interestingly, teachers in government schools are hired for the full twelve-month term, with one month holiday, while the other time is given over to attending university, carrying on research, and working on curriculum committees. The teachers in private schools are not government employees and thus do not receive the same salary, bursaries for upgrading credentials, or summer salaries.

Nursery Schools

Guarderia Infantil (nursery schools), formerly under the Department of Health and Welfare, are now under the jurisdiction of the Department of Education. Children from three months to six years are enrolled. The teachers are required to take the kindergarten teacher education course, but the objectives are oriented more toward custodial care and the improvement of health, since these are the children of working mothers and in many cases appear underprivileged. At six, they are normally enrolled in the *primaria* (elementary school).

CURRICULUM

In 1951, the kindergartens operated a program that included the following features:

1. a three year program that met the needs of the four-, five- and six-year-old children prior to enrollment in the primary school;
2. the extensive use of the outdoor environment, which enabled the school to enroll as many as 900 children in a single kindergarten complex;
3. an emphasis on real-life activities centered around experiences encountered in the home and in the specific social environment from which the children were drawn;
4. an emphasis on creative expression in movement, art, drama, music, and oral communication; and

5. the extensive involvement of parents in the program; for instance, mothers would come to the kindergarten in the afternoon to learn the basics of caring for the physical and social needs of their children.

Enthusiastic and committed teachers and directors placed emphasis on health, hygiene, recreation, patriotism, creative expression in the arts, and activities that emphasized the importance of love and respect for members of the family, the school, and the larger community.

Current Objective

The objective of the three-year kindergarten is presented as "the harmonious development of the integrated personality through the cognitive, affective, psychomotor domains coupled with the areas of language and the social environment." The aim is to achieve this through a sequential and spiral series of learning activities adapted to the developmental needs, abilities, and interests of the children at each of the three preschool grades. These learning experiences are organized around the needs of the child, the nature of the Mexican society, the knowledge deemed essential for coping at each stage of development, and preparation for success in primary school.

Areas Covered by the Program

The suggested tasks might well be viewed as developmental with the children to select those experiences that will meet the needs of the individual at his/her stage of development as well as provide group experiences from which a total group may benefit.

Centers of interest. Learning experiences are organized around centers of interest. The organizing centers that form the basis of the curriculum are those that grow out of the children's own needs, interests, concerns, questions, and problems as well as those specific areas of knowledge that are important from a cultural aspect.

Among the centers of interest dealt with on an expanding basis of sophistication and complexity are

    —bridging the gap between the home and the school
    —the child and his body

—holidays and special events, fiestas, games in Mexico and other countries

—traditions and Mexican heritage

—native animals and their usefulness to man

—communication, conversation, discussion, art, music, and written expression

—dramatization, puppetry, movement, rhythms band and games

—the child and his social world

—nutrition, cooking, food preparation

—literature and art as vehicles of creativity

—appreciation of native art and culture

—health and safety

At one time, Mexico had such a highly centralized system of kindergarten education that throughout the country the identical center of interest from the large number of suggested units available in their curriculum guides was cooperatively developed with their classes.

Curriculum development. Teachers are also continuously involved with personnel from the Research Center and the Preschool Department in curriculum development as an in-service activity during holidays and summers. At times, substitutes come in and take over while teachers meet in a local committee to plan and develop curricula. Besides these local meetings, intraschool committees and interstate conference and planning sessions assist in developing curriculum guides. Since there are three grades or levels— one for each kindergarten year—behavioral objectives as well as suggested activities, materials, and media for their implementation are included in the curriculum guide. Although every teacher is presented with a curriculum guide, the final decision as to what will be taught is the responsibility of the teacher, who determines this by what she knows about the strengths and weaknesses, the abilities and interests, and the needs and aspirations of her pupils. The type of kindergarten, the socio-economic status of the pupils, the location of the schools, and the abilities and strengths of the teachers as well as the instructional techniques and focus employed influence the choice of center of interest.

The creative teacher develops the child's psychomotor skills through play: cognitive ability through the use of such concepts as time, space, quantity, mathematics, and explorations of the environment; and affective domain through emphasis on social situations, interaction with planned perceptual experiences, and respect for the feelings of others. Opportunities for creativity are emphasized throughout as an avenue for the young child to reach the fullest potential as a whole human being.

Emphasis on the Individual

In Mexico in the 1950s, no children with problems of any type were found in the schools. To the query, "What about children with special needs—learning disabilities, problems in speech or hearing etc.?" the answer was invariably, "We have no such children in Mexico. Parents give their children so much love and affection that there are no problems with expression or communication." Further investigation, however, proved that with the crowded conditions at every educational level, any child with special needs was not admitted to a kindergarten or primary school.

All that has changed. Those who wish to teach children with special needs are now required, in addition to the regular four-year kindergarten teacher training program, to take an additional year of courses at the University of Mexico together with their cognate courses and practicum, working with children both in the preschool classroom and at the Research Laboratory under the supervision of qualified personnel.

Emphasis on the individual has brought about changes in enrollment. The current policy is to limit the number of children enrolled in a kindergarten to 200, or at most 300, rather than 900 as it formerly was. Also, the number of children assigned to one teacher has been reduced to a maximum of twenty-five, in order for the teacher to be able to discover the specific talents, needs, and interests and, if necessary, refer children to the proper agency for specialized training. In the words of the Director of Research and Development: "Today we go beyond the joy of discovery to the satisfaction of problem solving. The problems in our society are more complex than they were even a decade ago; therefore, the children must be equipped with skills which will enable them to solve our problems of communication and social awareness. We begin this development in the preschool by organizing the integrated spiral curriculum."

Typical Daily Programs

A brief study of a typical daily program as operated by two different schools will provide some insight into the relationship between the teacher and her pupils and focus in on how the educational policy is actually put to work.

A mixed socio-economic kindergarten. Some of the children came from homes of a high socio-economic level while others came from impoverished families. They were all enrolled in heterogeneous groups—fast and slow learners—in harmony with the philosophy of creating a lifelike situation in the *Jardin de Niños* (kindergarten). A total of 275 children were enrolled in this school, which was located on a beautiful landscaped site with a great deal of outdoor space for activities and play. Children were divided into seven groups, with about thirty-nine per teacher.

According to their ages, various children were involved in a variety of activities. The youngest group, the three- to four-year-olds enjoyed a twenty-five-minute story, well told by a teacher who had specialized in that area while at the university. At the end of the story, the children spontaneously participated in telling what they had liked best and why.

One five-year-old group was outdoors engaged in a rhythms class. To the sound of a recording, the children participated spontaneously and joyously in the rhythms and games—some directed by the teacher and some being their own creations.

Another five-year-old group was involved in some music activity. They thoroughly enjoyed singing both folk songs and patriotic hymns.

The only evidence of workbooks was with the six-year-old group in the third grade of kindergarten. They participated in a specially developed mathematics program. The units were based on concepts of measurement that related mathematical symbols and vocabulary to certain models. The children would use these models prior to working in their workbooks. Two more books were worked through prior to moving into the first grade where they were required to enroll at seven years of age.

There was a special gym teacher who came to the kindergarten twice a week. On other days, outdoor play was scheduled under the direction of a teacher who was encouraged to use the curriculum guide as just that; "a guide."

Individual creative writing was encouraged, but no actual handwriting lessons were given. Teachers were to create an environment and a program that took into consideration the strengths and weaknesses of both children and teacher.

A lower socio-economic school. In contrast with the previously mentioned kindergarten, which was located in an attractive suburb of the Mexican metropolis, this preschool was situated in what can be termed "an impoverished low-income area." The physical plant differed little from the other school, but there the similarity ended.

In this low-income neighborhood, the enrollment was larger, with 430 children in seven groups with small classes. In addition to the thirteen regular class teachers, there were a gym teacher, two special education teachers, each with a group of eleven children who had been diagnosed at the clinic as requiring special teaching, and a teacher doing her practice teaching while studying at the University of Mexico.

Here the emphasis was on developing harmonious relationships between the home, the school, and the community. There was also a conscious effort on the part of teachers to interest community children in the kindergarten program. Activities were geared to specific age groups.

The three-year-olds engaged in outdoor play with a sandbox, sand toys, a jungle gym, blocks, a doll house, balls, old tires and other outdoor equipment. After the outdoor session, they went directly to the easels for an art lesson.

The four-year-olds assumed the duties of street cleaners, since this was essential in this part of the city. Wearing hard hats they vigorously cleaned the streets. On completion of this task they spend some time in the swimming pool. In order to accommodate all the groups, swimming, which is an integral part of many kindergartens, is on the curriculum once a week for each group, with a gym teacher and a regular teacher in charge.

Two five-year-old groups went to the market to buy ingredients for making soup and fruit salad. They were accompanied by a student teacher, the regular teacher, and two parents. At the market, they made their choice of food, then bartered for it before paying as they had seen their parents do. When this group got back to school, they made soup on their electric stoves.

The six-year-olds spent their time working with problems in mathematics. After that twenty-four-minute period, the children eagerly participated in their art lesson, presenting a play using the puppets they had made. They also had their own vegetable garden, which they would later harvest when the center of interest was nutrition. At the end of the morning, each group gathered in its own classroom and planned the next day's activities as an incentive to return to the school. This plan is successful in motivating children to come back and continue working on the problems and centers of interest under way in the development of the unit.

An emphasis on such themes as safety, nutrition, cleanliness, cooking, and gardening is especially important in the lower socio-economic areas. The flexibility of the schedule accommodates varying distributions of time, personnel, specialized teachers, and creativity. The director is responsible for planning with the teachers, and the teacher then works out daily lesson plans as well as long-range unit plans.

CONCLUSION

In an area in which the motivation for learning must come largely from the teachers, it is essential that the curriculum be flexible to permit each teacher to work with the children she teaches. The emphasis on knowing children and attempting to meet their individual as well as group needs has added a new dimension to kindergarten education in Mexico.

The Mexican kindergarten teachers have always been a special group. They have always been committed to educating the youngest citizens. Now they have added knowledge of child development, psychology, and concern for the uniqueness of each child to their commitment and zealous guidance.

The emphasis on the creative potential of each child through a program that balances concern for development of the psychomotor, the affective, and cognitive domains in an environment in which there is freedom to express, time to explore, question, probe, and create over a three-year span prior to enrollment in the primary school provides the child with a firm foundation for future experiences as well as the excitement and joy of learning that initially characterize his attitudes toward school. This is possible to a greater degree in a program in which the years of early childhood extend from the three-year preschool to what we normally think of as the second year of primary school—the second grade.

The evolution of the Mexican kindergarten may well take as its motto "Past is Prologue" as it continues to provide a three-year education for an ever increasing percentage of the population—both urban and rural—in order that the diversity of the country becomes a factor that through communication of its various groups brings unity in understanding.

REFERENCES

Logan, Lillian M.: *Kindergarten Education in Mexico*, Ph.D. Dissertation. University of Wisconsin, Madison, 1952.
————. Kindergarten Education in Mexico. Wlla Victoria Bobbs Award Winning Studies, 1953, in *Education Horizons, 32:*206-207, Spring, 1954.
————. *Teaching the Young Child.* Boston, Houghton-Mifflin, 1960.

Chapter 9

EARLY CHILDHOOD EDUCATION
IN SWEDEN

BERNARD M. LALL and GEETA R. LALL

INTRODUCTION

IN Sweden, a country where there are 300,000 children under ten years of age whose mothers work more than fifteen hours a week, preschool facilities have long been regarded as a service to the family (Stenholm, 1970).

Formerly, child-care centers were regarded as a sort of poor relief for children of working mothers. Today they are looked upon as an essential service under proper and qualified supervision that teach children fundamental social skills before they enter structured schools.

The main emphasis in these centers is on the child's personal and social development, one complementing the other. Children learn to interact with others, develop a community feeling, take care of themselves, and prepare for the requirements of the first years of school life (Karre, 1973).

It is felt that the preschool can fulfill a special function in the development of the child. First of all, it brings children together from different environments, it teaches them to play and associate together, it develops their vocabulary, it provides experiences of the world around them, and it evens out social differences for the child (Stenholm, 1970).

Although the aims of these preschools have not yet been formulated, it is beginning to be regarded as an educational as much

123

as a social phenomenon (Stenholm 1970).

The Swedish philosophy of early childhood education is based on the theories of Arnold Gesell, Jean Piaget, and Erik Erikson. From these sources, teachers learn the concept of epigenesis, the proper rate and sequence for normal development. Their teaching approach resembles the British infant schools "discovery method." Their purpose is to provide an environment that is socially and physically stimulating. In this environment, children, unpressured, will discover their world.

Children are free to experiment and explore on their own, with adult guidance when needed. They are provided with the necessary skills for social interaction with peers and significant others.

Nursery education, according to the National Board of Education, should "complement and supplement homes to train to adjustment, cooperation and solidarity with a bigger group than the family" (Mueller, 1971).

Historical Development

Alva Myrdal, a pioneer in Swedish preschool education, founded the first training college for nursery school teachers in Stockholm to "provide training for the staff of the nursery schools that for pedagogical reasons had been set up by a municipal housing association" (Karre, 1973).

It was not until the 1960s that these ideas began to be formulated into a working program. Nursery schools have not been in existence very long, even though children do not start regular school until they are aged seven. For a long time, those responsible for the reforms in the educational system were oblivious to the importance of the preschool years. The time for reform arrived, and a government commission was set up for this purpose (Karre, 1973).

Objectives

The purpose of the preschool is to complement the family in offering every child optimal conditions for its social, emotional, physical, and intellectual development. The development of the child's personality is regarded as extremely important. During the early years, it is particularly important that each child should establish an inner security and be put in a position to learn cooperation with others.

The child has to learn good habits, self-help skills, and respect for rules and prohibitions. Fine and gross motor skills are developed as well as the ability to communicate effectively with others.

The Board of Education recommends that buildings and room arrangements should have the atmosphere of the child's home. They are to function as an extension of the home rather than as a school. They have to function in a group with others and need to have a knowledge of conditions outside the home, which can be obtained through field trips and excursions.

Formal preparation for school is the least emphasized portion of the preschool curriculum, and little provision is made for actual instruction. Children instead need preparation for the later social demands of school life. Personality and self-concept development, together with growing independence, are the main goals.

To accomplish these objectives, day care centers offer the following opportunities for development:

1. Physical-sensory stimulation—there is time and opportunity to cuddle, pat, and fuss over the child
2. Physical-motor stimulation—children have ample room and freedom to move about
3. Social stimulation—children have lots of attention from both adults and older children
4. Cognitive stimulation—children are talked with and given opportunities for speech development
5. Perceptual stimulation—there are materials and opportunities for many different sensory impressions
6. Emotional stimulation—the children know that caretaking people are fond of them (Mueller, 1971).

ORGANIZATION AND ADMINISTRATION OF THE E.C.E. PROGRAMS

Preschools are a voluntary effort of the local authorities, but are strongly encouraged by the state. The involvement of the Swedish central and local government authorities in preschool activities has greatly increased in the last few decades.

The supreme authority for all preschool activities is the Ministry of Health and Social Affairs. The National Board of Health and Welfare, under the ministry's jurisdiction, does the actual supervision of these schools. The County Administration is the regional authority, and at the local level, the Child Welfare Committees or Social Services Committees, a branch of the municipality, are ultimately responsible for these centers.

The National Board of Health publishes instructions and directives for local and other authorities as to how they can best operate the preschool centers.

In principle, anyone can set up preschools and can obtain government funding provided that the local committees approve the proposed plans. Thus one might find preschools operated by an association, a company, a church group, or a person. On the whole, however, most nursery schools are run by the local authority.

The full-day preschool should have a head teacher plus two preschool teachers for each department. The ratio of staff to children over two has to be 1:5. If infants are catered for, the ratio is 1:4. Where children have special needs that have to be met, the ratio is even lower. If a shortage of preschool teachers occurs, their place can be filled by nursery nurses.

In a part-day preschool, the staff to student ratio is 1:40 for children aged five to six and 1:30 for younger children. The ratio in leisure schools is 1:15.

The staff turnover is very low, and since women are allowed six months maternity leave, they do not have to give up their jobs on account of childbirth. The staff are usually in their early twenties (Mueller, 1971).

Types of Schools

Preschool institutions are organized along different lines.

Day nurseries. These cater for children from the ages of six months to seven years. Their parents are usually at work or studying or perhaps in need of a baby-sitter for a short period of time. They operate from 6:30 a.m. to 7:00 p.m. during the week and from 6:30 a.m. to 2:30 p.m. on Saturdays. They are closed on Sundays.

Nursery schools. These cater to children aged three to six and are open for not more than three hours per day. *Common day nurseries* are included in this category. They are a combination of the day nurseries and play schools. The common day school can admit children for periods of varying duration, depending on the needs of the family. Children arrive and leave when they have to, some staying for the whole day, while others only spend the morning or the afternoon there (Karre, 1973).

Municipal family day nursery. These are nurseries run in private homes with the approval of the local authorities. These mainly function in a baby-sitting fashion. They cater to children with health problems.

Farming day nurseries. These provide full day care for children aged one through seven whose parents' work in the fields during harvest time. They are organized and operated by the rural districts. The most serious problem with these schools is the recruitment of qualified teachers for the short harvest period. Since it coincides with school holidays in Northern Sweden, qualified staff can be found, but there still remains a shortage. The success of the summer program in some areas has led to a year long preschool program for which it is much easier to find qualified staff.

Recreation centers. These cater to children who have nobody at home to look after them when nursery school lets out for the day. Only the youngest children are accommodated.

The majority of children under seven who have working parents are supervised in the home, with the next largest number in private family day nurseries. The rest are served in day nurseries, nursery schools, and local authority family day nurseries (Karre, 1971).

Financing

The cost of preschools is shared among the state, the municipality, and the parents. The state contributes 35 percent of the cost, local authorities approximately 50 percent, and the parents the rest.

The state provides an initial grant of SKr 6,000* per place, plus a loan of SKr 4,000 per place (1973) unless it is built with a state housing loan. These funds are not provided for part-day pre-

---

* 1 SKr (Swedish Krone) = (approx.) 22 cents U.S.

school centers. Grants for part-day centers can be obtained from the State Inheritance Fund.

The National Board of Health and Welfare approves and pays initial grants, while loans are approved by the Board and paid by the National Office for Administrative Rationalization and Economy. Operating grants are provided by the State for institutions that are open for at least five hours per day. These grants comprise about 25 percent of the cost per child and are approved and paid by the Board. It is assumed that those centers receiving grants have properly qualified management personnel and that the facilities are adequate for the child's needs.

Parents pay according to their income, the number of children in day care, and family size. However, the cost cannot exceed SKr 20 ($4) per day for day nurseries. The monthly fee for preschools is from SKr 20-40 ($4-8), with certain municipalities offering free services. Leisure centers charge from SKr 10-30 ($2-6) per month.

Organization of New Centers

The expansion of child care centers has been given continued attention by the minister for Family Affairs. Continued priority is being given to populous areas and developing industrial districts. This emphasis on centers can be seen in the fact that of all the child care centers in Sweden, Stockholm has 30 percent of the day nursery enrollment, 25 percent of the nursery school enrollment, and 50 percent of the free time centers' enrollment.

Impetus for the expansion of child care centers has come from the Central Committee for Cooperation, organized in 1963. Its membership represents many influential bodies, such as the Board of Education, the Labor Market Board, the Swedish Trade Union Confederation, etc. This committee sponsors studies that determine the factors involved in the planning and building of child care centers. On the local level, county committees have the responsibility for the development of child centers in their geographic areas.

Their aim is to provide enough facilities so that parents who wish to place their children in a center will have an appropriate type of day care program available to them. The State government, as an incentive to local authorities, offers loans and subsidies for the development of child centers. Grants for the operation of day nurseries equals 20 percent of the operating costs and 18 percent of the operating costs for extended day care.

New centers can be set up by public and private groups, a combination of public and private groups, or individual organizations. Examples of such centers and their sponsoring organizations are as follows:

CENTER	TYPE	SPONSOR
Forsberg's Minnie	Day nursery	Private family
Tuna Stugan	Combined day nursery, preschool, and free time school	Student Union
The Lazarett	Day nursery	Hospital
Rodd Stugan	Day nursery	Factory
Bjorkhagens	Day nursery	Municipality
Morgonsol	Day nursery	Salvation Army

Voluntary organizations that do not receive a public subsidy do not have to follow the state rules and regulations.

These centers, depending on their sponsors, are situated in a variety of locations. Factory or hospital centers are located at the places of need, and student unions have theirs close to universities.

Selection of Recipients of Day Care

Local child welfare committees have the responsibility for determining which children need day care. The estimation of the number of children needing this care is done by the day care unit in the Social Bureau. Child allowance records* are used as a starting point, and personal interviews are also conducted. No entrance requirements need to be met, and waiting lists for placement are extremely long. Registration usually takes place at birth, but because of the shortage of centers, only about 50 percent of six-year-olds are in child care centers of any kind.

There are more preschools than nurseries. Children are admitted between the ages of four and seven, but the majority attending

---

*Families receive an annual allowance for each child until the child turns sixteen.

are six-year-olds. Even though there are no eligibility requirements for admission, the ratio of demand to supply leads to the establishment of priorities—children of working mothers, single parents, students, and disabled mothers are given preference.

Health

Health checks are done on children before admission. Children, if they have not been immunized earlier, are treated now. Dental care is also administered. If children become ill while at the center, their parents are notified, and the child is isolated in a sick room until he can go home.

Personnel are available to help working parents when their children are sick. If parents cannot leave work to fetch their sick child, these workers will transport the child home and care for him until his parents get home. These workers will even perform this nursing function on weekends if parents have to work then. They are recruited and selected by Home Health Committees who arrange training courses for them.

Exceptional Children

Three day care nurseries for emotionally disturbed children are provided, together with one day nursery for physically handicapped children.

The centers' physician or teachers make referrals to the district social worker or to the child welfare worker in the central Social Bureau. Psychologists are contacted, and they work with the child and his family. These psychologists and other case workers make recommendations to the central Day Care Unit for the placement of deviant children in appropriate child care centers.

Family Day Nurseries

Social workers from day care centers make regular visits to the childrens' homes. They serve as the link between parents and the day care centers.

Day Care mothers are paid by the day at the rate of $2.70 per hour (1971) taxable, and given a dollar a day for food, which is nontaxable. They also receive holiday pay, health insurance, and a pension. They must take a ninety hour course in child care and they receive a stipend for attendance at such a course. They participate in parent-teacher meetings and child care conferences so that they may learn more about the philosophy of child care.

"The Three-Child System"

In this system three children from three different homes are looked after by a nurse who uses one home each week on a rotating basis. Food for the nurse and the children is provided by the parents whose home is being used. Parents pay the usual day care fee on a sliding scale basis. The home being used should have adequate facilities and sufficient space. The nurse's salary and traveling expenses are paid by the Social Bureau. The cost of such a system is approximately SKr 10-15 less per day than costs per day for group care.

PROGRAMS AND FACILITIES AT DAY CARE CENTERS

In describing the program and facilities used at the day nurseries, we will use the *Forsberg's Minnie* day nursery, which is a typical example of the day nurseries in Sweden.

It is located in the midst of a new development of single and two-family homes about a mile from downtown Lund in the South of Sweden. The Center is in a one-story red brick building designed especially for this purpose, similar in style to the homes surrounding it. The building and furnishings, many toys, and all durable equipment were donated as a Forsberg family memorial but the operating budget is provided by the Social Bureau of Lund. Building specifications meet state requirements, and the program is directly supervised by a professionally educated social worker in the Day Care Unit of the Social Bureau.

This Center accommodates 48 children:
1. Eight in the one-to-two year group.
2. Ten in the two-to-three year group.
3. Twelve to fifteen in the three-to-five year group.
4. Eighteen to twenty in the five-to-seven year group.

These groups or departments are staffed by
1. Two nursery nurses for the eight babies.
2. One preschool teacher and one nurse for ten two- to three-year-olds.
3. Two preschool teachers for twelve to fifteen three- to five-year olds.

4. Two preschool teachers for eighteen to twenty five- to seven-year-olds.

In addition to teachers and nurses, staff includes the director or headmistress, two kitchen staff, and maintenance workers.

Children arrive from 6:30 a.m. but not later than 10:30 a.m. Places are reserved for children who need them regularly for at least five hours everyday. Breakfast is served between 7:00 a.m. and 8:00 a.m. It varies every day and typically consists of cereal, yogurt, milk, bread, and butter.

After breakfast, it is time for free play. For children three and older, the half-hour between 10:00 and 10:30 a.m. is for group activity, singing or playing games, led by the teacher. For children under three, this group activity lasts for only five or ten minutes. Activities are "flexible, depending on the children's interest."

Lunch is at 11:30 at an unhurried pace, a time for learning as well as eating. Afterward, the children clear and wipe off the table and rinse dishes. A lot of talking goes on all the time with much warm encouragement by adults. Children are taught to manipulate utensils and are allowed to feed themselves as much or as little food as they want with no concern for the mess and no coercion.

Naptime is 12:30. There is a quiet corner for the older children if they do not wish to nap, but all of them must be in the sleeproom for about ten minutes at the beginning of naptime. After that, they may get up and play quietly if they are not sleepy. Cots slide upended into wall closets much as trays are stored in kitchen cupboards. They are easily folded up and put away after naptime.

All children brush their teeth and have a story before naptime. Stories may be accompanied by home-made picture books.

From about two o'clock, activities are going again. In good weather the children go outdoors. Each department has its own fenced-in play yard with indoor-outdoor carpeting and a common garden for growing vegetables that the children plant, harvest, and eat. Except for the babies, each department also has its own kitchen and a workshop, each scaled to the appropriate size. The children do a lot of cooking and baking, some of it for their lunches, using recipe books made of pictures. Boys as well as girls cook and girls use the workshop. There is a great emphasis on minimizing sex role differences.

Each unit has two playrooms, one of which includes the kitchen, a workshop, a lavatory scaled to size, storage space for materials and equipment, an office for staff, and an isolation room for sick children. The isolation room also has pets in cages and is set up as a "tea corner." When not in use for a sick child, anyone can go in to watch and help to feed and care for the animals.

Each child has his own cup, toothbrush, and towel in a separate open cupboard, which is marked with a fruit sticker to identify it for him. Each baby has his towels, diapers, and changes of clothing in a separate closed cupboard to guard against infection. There are small toilets for the youngest children, and all toilets have grates over the open seats to keep the toddlers from slipping in and being frightened.

The possibilities for activity are varied. In addition to sand and water play, cooking, and "shop," there is finger-painting, clay, and rhythm instruments for the children, negro and white dolls of all sizes and doll clothes, playhouse corners properly furnished, construction and stacking blocks in varying sizes, wheeled-toys to push, pull, or ride, and slides and climbing apparatus both indoors and outdoors. For the babies, there are carriages and strollers, cribs to nap in, windows down to the floor to look out of, a milk kitchen, and a diaper changing room. Children change into play clothes when they arrive and clothing can be washed and dried on the premises. Both indoors and outside there is space for running, rolling, crawling, hiding, climbing, grouping, and being alone. Everywhere there are interesting things to touch, feel, hear, and see. There are collages all over; the walls are decorated with them in bright and soft colors and lots of different textures. Interior walls are made of brick and a variety of woods. Floors are vinyl tile. Every room has large windows for air and sunshine and views. Walls are yellow, orange, blue, or green; they are decorated with cork, burlap, flannel, seeds, snapshots, and felt animals – all sorts of shapes, sizes, textures and colors. Mobiles are child-made.

The children are quite at liberty to draw and paint and work with clay or water. They use large newsprint a yard wide and five feet long and fist-sized crayons. They run around barefooted; they ride tractors, wheel trucks, push a wooden train on a wooden track, sweep up the playhouse and rearrange large size doll furniture in the doll corner. There are many stuffed animals, small and carryable, huge and dragable. Everything is washable and colorful and flowers are everywhere. They grow profusely indoors and outdoors and are cut for each small table.

The five- and six-year-olds move freely in and out of the fenced-in play yard but are watched carefully. From 2:00 p.m. parents come to get the children, but most come around 5 o'clock (Mueller, 1971).

SUMMARY

Swedish nursery schools serve to supplement the nuclear family. The care given in these schools should be comparable to that given in the home. The buildings and rooms are thus furnished and arranged in such a way as to convey a homelife appearance and atmosphere. They thus function as an extension of the home, not just as a school.

The demand for preschools is greater than the supply. Presently, efforts are being made to meet this demand. Volunteer groups are encouraged to establish centers and are subsidized by the state if they need funding. Local authorities should offer all children the possibility of attending preschool for at least two years.

"With the view gaining acceptance in Sweden that children need both the preschool and the home, it is unreasonable to demand that parents meet all the child's needs" (Karre, 1973). "In fact, it is now recognized that children may have needs beyond those provided for in a pleasant home environment" (Mueller, 1971). Thus it becomes the responsibility of both the parents and the community to provide for these needs.

REFERENCES

Karre, Marianne, et. al.: Social rights in Sweden before school starts, *Child Care-Who Cares.* New York, Basic Books, Inc., 1973.

Kerr, Anthony: *Schools of Europe.* London, Bowes and Bowes, 1960.

Mueller, Jeanne. *Pre-school Education and Day Care for Swedish Children.* Swedish Information Service, 1971.

Paulston, Rolland G.: *Educational Change in Sweden: Planning and Accepting the Comprehensive School Reforms*. New York, Teachers College Press, 1968.

Rosengren, Bodil: *Pre-school in Sweden: Facts, Trends and Future*. Stockholm, The Swedish Institute, 1973.

The Swedish Institute: Primary and secondary education in Sweden, *Fact Sheets on Sweden*. Stockholm, The Swedish Institute, March, 1975.

Chapter 10

EARLY CHILDHOOD EDUCATION IN NORWAY

LISA HEBER ØSTLYNGNEN

INTRODUCTION

BEFORE discussing early childhood education in Norway, one first needs to learn something about Norway and its people.

Norway is situated in Northern Europe, with one third of the country reaching above the Arctic Circle. The coastal areas enjoy a mild climate because of the Gulf Stream, whereas the interior has very cold winters and really hot summers. Norway is about the size of Italy, long and narrow with an extensive coastline and many fjords.

The country has approximately four million people, with about 50 percent living in towns and cities, the rest being spread out throughout the country. Next to Iceland, Norway's population density is the lowest in Europe.

Philosophy. Regarding philosophy, colleges and other teacher training institutions have taught the ideas and theories of Rousseau, Pestalozzi, Froebel, Decroly, Kilpatrick, and Montessori. Susan Isaacs and Jean Piaget were first heard about in the 1940s, and after World War II, Gesell gained recognition. Teachers in early childhood education have been advised to select the best ideas from these different theorists.

Teachers of young children are trained for every age group under seven years of age, which is the compulsory school entrance age in Norway. During the first few years of life, it is difficult to

136

distinguish between caring and education, thus child psychology, education, nutrition, et cetera has to be combined during this period. Research has shown that nutritional deficiencies in the early years can have a lifelong impact. In addition, the child's need for affection and security have to be met, and they need to be accepted by their peers and also by adults. They also need to gain independence and self-respect. These are some of the main points in the Norwegian philosophy of early childhood education.

Instead of thinking of education and using the term in a normal sense, we should adopt the view of Dr. Mary Essex who, at the World Conference for Early Childhood Education in Washington, D.C., in 1968, said, "We should have respect for the nurture of all children." Nurture in this sense means "The act or process of raising or promoting the development of; training; rearing; upbringing" (Webster, 1960). Dr. Essex called early childhood educators the nurturing profession, and this viewpoint is in harmony with the Norwegian philosophy of early childhood education.

Objectives. In June 1975, Norwegian law made provision for *Barnehager*. This word, derived from Froebel, means kindergarten, but the law added a new dimension to its meaning. Before this law was passed, the word *barnehage* referred to a school for children between three and seven years of age. Day care centers for children under three had a different name. Today, because of the 1975 law, *barnehage* refers to all kinds of provisions for children from birth to age seven as long as it is directed or supervised by trained teachers. It could be any of the following:

1. a day care center for children four months to seven years old, or
2. a teacher- or parent-operated group with ten to fifteen children, supervised by a trained teacher, open for as little as six hours per week, or
3. four to six family day care set-ups supervised by a trained teacher.

The objectives of these kinds of early childhood programs are outlined in paragraph two of the regulations as follows: The *Barnehage* shall give children a good environment with emphasis on play and social experiences with other children and with adults. The *Barnehage* shall develop each child's personality, help children to develop tolerance and the ability to care for each other, and provide children with developmental opportunities through different kinds of play and activity experiences. In cooperation with the home, the *Barnehage* shall contribute in providing an environment that will guarantee individual and group care and support, stimulation, development and learning, and ethical guidance.

Early childhood education in Norway provides for parent involvement, thus emphasis is put on preserving and perpetuating the traditional culture that has been handed down from generation to generation.

ORGANIZATION AND ADMINISTRATION OF E.C.E. PROGRAMS

Paragraphs three and four of the *Barnehage* law states that it is the responsibility of the local communities to provide children with opportunities for growth by establishing and operating *barnehager* or by giving financial support to establish and maintain such set-ups. The community shall also draw up a program-plan for establishing *barnehager*. According to the law, facilities already in operation will be studied and a rationale describing the need for such facilities will be formulated. Any areas of need would be provided for, including the establishment of new set-ups. Special emphasis should be put on differentiating the set-ups offered. The program-plan shall state priorities and set a time-table for establishing new set-ups. The cost should be approved by the community council.

Early Childhood Programs in Norway may vary in structure according to the different needs of the various communities. Different kinds of programs may even be found in one community. These programs may be privately operated to provide for a particular need among a few families. A company or a hospital may also establish day care centers for the children of their employees. A housewives organization or church group may also decide to organize a program.

Whoever the founders of these programs are, they all have to follow the *Barnehager* law. The ministry of Consumers and Administration provides guidelines as to the organization of the various programs and requires that the program leaders keep in touch with them. Where federal subsidies are provided, the ministry may require certain conditions of the various programs, including a program-plan for development.

Even though programs for early childhood education come under the jurisdiction of the Ministry of Consumers and Administration and not the Ministry of Education, some of the programs may use the facilities of local schools, be it a day care program for teachers' children or an ordinary day care set-up. However, these programs are not part of the educational system in Norway in which the Ministry of Education only deals with the regular school, starting at age seven. Even then, *care* and *stimulation* are emphasized in the preschool years and early childhood education is viewed as a value in itself, not as a forerunner to compulsory education.

Administration. Each community elects its own Early Childhood committee, which is responsible for the planning, building, and operation of all early childhood programs in that community. Norway consists of nineteen counties, and each county employs a County Supervisor who is in charge of these programs. The Early Childhood Committee consists of seven or eight members. It must include the County Supervisor, a representative of the employees in each *barnehage* in the community and one parent representative.

The duties of the Early Childhood Committee include the following:

— Follow up and carry out decisions the Community Council has approved according to the law for *Barnehager*.
— Work out a program-plan for the development of *barnehager* and present it to the Community Council.
— Submit suggestions for early childhood education programs and regulations for *Barnehager* run by the community to the Community Council and approve regulations for private set-ups and *barnehager* run by companies and public institutions.
— Forward applications for approval of programs to the federal authorities.
— Approve annual plans for the operation of programs.
— Supervise programs in the community and see to it that the programs are operated in accordance with laws, regulations,

rules, and community approval.
- Cooperate with authorities and others whose activities are connected to the *barnehager*, i.e. the school board, the social committee, the child·welfare committee, the health council, etc.
- Outline the Early Childhood Committee's responsibilities.
- Offer suggestions regarding the budget for early childhood programs in the community.
- Submit suggestions to the Community Council regarding tuition in the *barnehager*, where the community completely or partly covers the deficit.
- Approve appointment of personnel in *barnehager*.
- Approve applications to *barnehager* on the basis of nomination by the local board.

There are many decisions that can be made by the Early Childhood Committee. However, when it comes to the program-plan for new set-ups, the approved program-plan is sent by the Early Childhood Committee to the county, after which it goes to the Ministry for Consumers and Administration where it is licensed.

As far as funding is concerned, the Early Childhood programs get subsidies from the local community as well as from the ministry. The subsidized amount varies according to the number of hours during which a *barnehage* operates.

In 1977, the ministry paid 200 dollars per child in day care centers and set-ups operating six to fifteen hours weekly, and 350 dollars per child for those facilities operating sixteen to thirty hours per week. For children under three years of age, the ministry paid 1000 dollars per child in centers operating more than thirty hours weekly and 700 dollars per child for those over the age of three. In addition, the ministry provides extra funding to new programs during the first five years of operation. Programs that integrate handicapped children also receive an extra 5 percent above the ordinary subsidies.

Programs run by the local communities will have their deficits covered; this usually also applies to programs operated by private organizations, etc.

Parents pay according to the number of hours the child attends the center, the amount varying between 50 and 80 dollars per month. Provision is also made for qualified children to attend free of charge. In the capital city of Oslo, approximately 50 percent of the children attending *barnehager* in 1977 did so tuition-free, their costs being paid by the community.

Several years ago, two types of day-care centers were in operation. One was open from four to six hours a day and accommodated children whose mothers had part-time jobs. These children were usually aged four to seven years old. A second type of center was open from eight to five and accepted children of single parents or children of parents who were both working. Presently, these two types of centers have merged into one type. Day-care centers now operate for nine to ten hours a day, and children arrive and leave when they need to.

TYPES OF CURRICULUM AVAILABLE FOR E.C.E. PROGRAMS

Day-care centers in Norway have traditionally provided children with care and attention comparable to that given them at home. According to law, additional stimulation and learning is also given. These centers have to provide opportunities for play, creative activities, excursions, etc.

During free play periods children have opportunities to choose activities according to their needs and interests. These may include block-building, toys such as Lego, peg-boards, and water pistols. Other activities include dressing up and other forms of role playing, woodwork, drawing, painting, modeling with clay, etc.

A certain portion of the day is set aside when all the children gather together in a circle with the teacher for singing, story-telling, discussions, and other related activities. A special time is also set aside for musical activities, exercise in a nearby gymnasium, or skiing in the water. The Skiing Association has arranged a special program for children aged five through seven that takes place during the day-care-center hours. The children ski for one hour twice a week over a period of six weeks. A nominal fee is paid by the parents.

In Norway, year round out-door play is stressed by parents, health authorities, as well as by personnel in day-care centers. Infants are placed, in a crib or baby carriage, on a roof-terrace. In winter, they are wrapped in fur-lined sleeping bags. Older children play outside, wearing snow suits in winter and plastic overalls, jackets, and southwests in rainy weather. By adding rubber boots to their other apparel, they can enjoy playing in the water without getting soaked.

The free play periods may occur outdoors in summer and indoors in winter, although these may be combined according to the childrens' needs and interests.

Children who arrive at the center early may receive breakfast. Lunch is served in the middle of the day and a meal is also served near the end of the day. Before a meal, children are allowed to go to the toilet and also to wash up for the meal. Older children use the toilet as needed, the younger ones at certain times. In the infant stage, they are individually taken care of.

Schedule of the program. Day-care center schedules are flexible, depending on the individual center and the children attending. However, a typical schedule follows this format:

1. Children are met by one of the staff members in the cloakroom. Parents undress their children, or children do so by themselves when their parents leave.
2. Breakfast is served in some day-care centers.
3. The free-play period follows next and lasts for as long as two to three hours. Story-telling may take place on an individual basis, or the children may go into another room to listen to music. Other special needs may also be attended to such as going to the store with an adult or helping in the kitchen.
4. Toilet, wash-up, and meal.
5. "Circle-time."
6. Out-door-play.
7. Extra meal.
8. Children leave.

In addition to regular day-care centers, other programs are offered for young children. For example, a group of ten to fifteen children may be funded by their parents and supervised by a trained teacher, and may have a program operating for as little as six hours a week. Such programs usually fill the needs in small communities that have a scattered population. Children may gather at a certain center two or three times a week for three hours.

The same teacher can conduct a program twice a week in one location and three times a week in another place. Sometimes the program only operates during special seasons, e.g. planting and harvesting times.

These flexible set-ups are subsidized by the ministry according to the number of operating hours, as mentioned before, but they have to be run by or supervised by a trained teacher. The schedule usually consists of a free play period with creative activities and music and "circle-time." Usually meals or snacks are served at the beginning and at the end of the three hours.

Another type of set-up may be a four to six family day-care center supervised by a trained teacher. In these set-ups, the maximum number of children is four, including the host family's own children. A supervising teacher coordinates this type of program. It is her responsibility to see that the children get proper care and stimulation. Play materials are provided and a subsidy is allotted by the ministry, along with funding by the community. In addition, the parents pay a fee that is equivalent to that paid in regular day-care centers. Children in family day-care centers are usually under three years of age, or they may include children whose health would suffer if they attended a conventional day-care center. The goals and objectives of all these programs are to provide the child with stimulation and care according to his needs and interests.

Handicapped children are integrated into regular day-care centers with the parents' permission. Allowances also have to be made for different cultural groups. In recent years, Norway has witnessed the influx of foreign workers, mostly from Pakistan, India, and Turkey. Originally the children of these workers attended regular day-care centers. Recently, though, new, smaller centers have been established where these young children can first learn their mother tongue and absorb their own culture before being integrated into the Norwegian day-care center. It has been proven that in this way the children do not go through an identity crisis, and they also learn better and easier.

In each type of early childhood education program, the child's individual needs are determined through observation of the child at play and through physical examination. Specialists from a guidance, speech, or health clinic are also involved in determining the child's needs. Team conferences are then held and decisions are made as to what actions need to be taken. During the regular daily program, the personnel at the center decide how best to serve the child's needs.

The teacher, whether in a day-care center or supervising a parent operated family day-care center, has the responsibility to see that the children are given proper care, stimulation, and ethical guidance as required by the regulations issued by the ministry. She is the authority in the field. She should not be authoritarian or domineering or permissive. Rather, she should function in a democratic way towards the children, parents, and her coworkers. She provides a conducive atmosphere and serves as a resource person.

There is no formal evaluation done as to the growth and achievement of children in these programs. No testing is done, except when consultation takes place at a child guidance center. Usually growth and development are evaluated on a weekly basis by the staff who use their observations of the children as an evaluative tool.

Regarding punishment, Norwegian law forbids corporal punishment in all schools, including early childhood education programs. The only type of punishment used in these programs is the removal of a child from a room when he has been disturbing the other children. Even then, he is still supervised by a grown-up in another room and may even join a different group of children. No rewards are offered; the children usually take turns doing special jobs which they like. Successful completion of the task is sufficient reward, along with teacher praise.

Provisions for children between zero and seven years are broken down into various levels.

Day care centers operating from 7:45 a.m. to 5 p.m. admit children from four months to seven years of age. The age groups are broken down as follows:

1. four months to one and a half years
2. one and a half to three years
3. three to five years
4. five to seven years

Sometimes these groupings are rearranged, thus one might have a group comprised of one- to seven-year-olds, or two- to seven-year-olds, the more common grouping being three- to seven-year-olds.

Organization and Schedule of Programs
Four Months to One and a Half Years

In this grouping, the whole atmosphere should be one filled with calmness, fondling, love, and warmth. There must be a deep understanding of the background of the individual child and his needs. The child's physiological needs are not the only needs to be satisfied. The child's psychological needs also need to be met. The child's present developmental state should be considered when planning programs and activities. Thus the program plans for
1. developing patterns of bodily independence and self-care;
2. encouraging motor activities and giving the child a feeling of self-reliance;
3. stimulating the senses and in that way the cognitive processes;
4. giving the child opportunities to have social and emotional contacts with adults trained for this type of work.

Developing Patterns of Bodily Independence and Self-Care

Within the framework of the infant nursery group, each child's needs, his rhythm, and habits are identified and attended to. When the infant, through crying or through other signs, expresses his psychological needs, the adult will try to find the reason for his behavior and will attempt to satisfy the child's needs. Cleanliness is not the only consideration in handling the child. Psychological factors such as warm hands and soft, confident movements on the part of the adult are stressed. When the child is fed he is held in close physical contact with the adult. Later, the child may be seated in a chair and allowed to feed himself morsels. At one year of age, he often uses his own spoon along with the adults and is allowed to practice feeding himself and drinking out of a mug. The crib and bedding should give the child sufficient security and allow him freedom to move and provide contact with his outer world.

Motor Activities. The child should be given optimal opportunities to exercise both his large and small muscles. To facilitate this, the surface of the bed or mattress, the child's position in bed, and his clothing must be adequate. The child should have the opportunity to exercise his muscles, to raise his head, chest, and shoulders from a prone position, to turn from side to side, from a prone position to a supine position and vice versa. The child should also be able to sit up, attempt to stand, and maybe even walk. Arms, hands, and fingers are exercised by giving the child an opportunity to grasp, release, bang things together, finger, point, or pick up things.

Stimulating the Senses and the Cognitive Processes. As thinking at this age is based, to a large extent, on previous experiences, it is very important that the environment provides the child with such experiences. The child learns about his environment through his senses, which need to be stimulated through suitable play materials and through meaningful social contact.

As the body develops, the child should be placed in different positions in order that he may observe his surroundings from various angles and different levels, thus stimulating his intellect. Stimulation is important at all times, not just during feeding and caretaking. Sufficient stimulation is necessary for language development.

Social and Emotional Contact. The near presence of a person who has a good emotional relationship with the child is just as important as giving the child suitable play materials. The adult who satisfies the child's physiological needs should also satisfy the child's psychological needs. Intimate adult contact with the child is brought about by holding the child, keeping good eye contact, showing a smiling face, using a low pleasant voice, chatting softly, and humming to the child. Since basic trust and confidence in other people is established in the first years of life, it is very important that enough time is available for individual contact with the same adult whenever needed. This significant adult also shows approval whenever the child achieves success in some task.

At this stage, children may view other children as rivals for the adults' affection and favor. If the children are gradually introduced to others at their own level with an adult nearby who can respond whenever necessary, they will slowly develop a positive feeling towards other children.

The Daily Program. The daily program in nurseries for the very young is not governed by regulations. Rather, the teacher has to be able to develop a daily schedule bearing in mind the type of environment, the individual children in the group, and the amount of time that the different children spend in the nursery, e.g. younger children need more meals and more sleep than older children. Children six to eighteen months usually have established their own daily rhythm that should be followed.

Programs for Children One and a Half to Three Years

At this stage, the teacher is the most important link between the home and the nursery. Through close adult contact and correct planning of the physical environment and the social and emotional climate, the children come to regard the nursery as a place where, in addition to the home, they can feel secure and well looked after.

The regular daily schedule and the sense of order give children at this age the security they seem to need. This program provides for

1. sufficient opportunities for tactile sensory exploration;
2. encouragement in motor activities and nurturing of autonomy and initiative; and
3. opportunities for good social and emotional contact with adults trained for this kind of work, as well as contact with other children.

Through close contact with adults, language develops, and through contact with other children at their own developmental level, the child will gradually enjoy being with his peers.

Sufficient Opportunities for Tactile Sensory Exploring. In this age group, the children are intrigued with the possibilities of coming into contact with various materials. Experiences with the materials themselves are the main consideration. The adult's contribution to organizing and stimulating the activity increases the child's interest and pleasure. Enough time, adequate space, and a rich supply of various kinds of materials are of great importance. Children come to know their surroundings through these tactile experiences and they should be allowed to experiment as much as possible. They learn to distinguish sizes, shapes, textures, etc. in this way.

Encouraging Motor Activities, Nurturing of Autonomy and Initiative. The physical facilities should be planned in order that the child has enough space in which to exercise. He should have enough opportunities to be able to exercise his large as well as his small muscles. Floor space in the play areas should, therefore, exceed the minimum size requirements. A rich and varied supply of materials will give the children opportunities to use their trunk muscles, their arms, fingers, and their eyes. They also obtain some knowledge as to the type of materials they are using.

The child should be suitably dressed so that he can move freely. Furniture should have curved edges so that the child does not hurt himself on corners. Chairs and tables should be of a height suitable to the child's size, i.e. their feet should rest on the floor when seated. By mastering different motor activities, the child at this age gains pleasure and achieves a certain measure of self-reliance.

The child exercises his body through these motor activities, and they help him obtain the practice he needs in skills such as jumping, walking, running, climbing, etc. These skills are a necessary part of his developmental process.

Children should have many opportunities to let things fall, and to slide, push, roll, float, throw, empty, fill, pull, and manipulate things. Experience such as putting things on top of each other, banging on drums, making sounds, and pointing to things help him obtain a knowledge of objects and actions.

Through active play, children have a way to get rid of their inner frustrations and other destructive impulses. This type of play channels aggression into hard work, e.g. use of pegboard, beating a drum, kicking a ball.

Providing Opportunities for Good Social and Emotional Contact. Equipment and play materials have an indirect influence upon the social group life. Ample floor space reduces the number of conflicts between children. It is important in this age group to have a duplication of each item in order to reduce fighting over materials.

The adult is important in that he structures the environment, is part of it, and is a role model for the children to emulate. The teacher and her assistants provide security by showing affection, caring, and interest and by praising the child for his successes. The adults provide help only when absolutely necessary, not before.

They also facilitate the gradual transition to new activities. When necessary, they set limits on the child's activities. The adults' example in a wide variety of socially acceptable behavior patterns will gradually be assimilated and emulated by the child. This includes showing sympathy, helpfulness, generosity, learning to take turns, borrowing, sharing, and exchanging play materials.

By playing·with their peers, children learn to understand themselves and each other. The adult plans activities that require group participation such as meals, naps, and simple singing games. Through these activities, children will feel at ease and will develop a sense of unity with others who are their own age or who are at the same developmental stage as they are.

Appropriate educational planning, opportune adult intervention and guidance, and demonstrations as to how social situations should be handled help direct the children to a positive social awareness. Play situations involving physical acts such as biting, hair pulling, pushing, pinching, and throwing objects at each other will gradually be replaced by cooperation and parallel play.

Social activities should be carefully planned and should be gradually and unobtrusively introduced into the daily program.

The Daily Program. In addition to regular care, meals, naps, etc., the children should have plenty of time for free play. During these periods, the child engages in activities that he likes best. The child chooses his own materials and selects his own activities, up to a certain point, without adult intervention.

The materials available and the child's experience and imagination are the bases upon which to build. The teacher supports and stimulates whenever needed and provides a secure and calm atmosphere. During free play periods, the child may play alone or with others. At this time, the teacher has a good opportunity to observe individual children and their relationship with materials and others.

During free play periods, individual activity materials are introduced. Creative activities, individually or collectively, experimentation, and movement play are also part of the free play period.

The child gets pleasure and gains self-respect when he is allowed to choose his play materials and his playmates. This is often expressed through joyous laughter and verbal exclamations. Sometimes simple imitative play may appear, and children can, through this play, learn something about social behavior patterns. Enough materials should be available to stimulate different kinds of play.

Group conversations are a natural outcome of interactional play. However for this age group, conversation consists, for the most· part, of adults talking with the children, interjecting with personal comments from their own experience. The focus for such conversations may be concrete objects, pictures, live animals, or some mutual experience that occurred that day. One of the purposes of such a conversation is to allow the child practice in listening to others and also to be able to communicate with those around him. The teacher may also introduce topics for discussion that will draw the children into the discussion. This stimulation of the child's language development is important. This can be enhanced by visits to places of interest, e.g. library, museum, store, kitchen, janitor. Being able to communicate effectively will help the child's personal development.

Music, Singing, and Rhythmical Play. Through music and singing, the child will gradually acquire the ability to listen effectively and will learn to use rhythms and different pitches. Through simple songs, nursery rhymes, folk tunes, singing games, and listening to music, children have an opportunity to experience the joy of music. They will learn to use their voices in such a way that singing and music will become a natural means of expression.

Rhythmic playing, listening games, and similar activities will develop the child's ability to concentrate. Music and singing are so compatible with movement play that they are readily combined for this age group. By moving according to music and through mimicry, the children use their bodies as a medium of expression. Movement play such as drumming, clapping hands, and marching may be of help in releasing pent-up feelings.

Intellectual Activities—Language Stimulation. By exploring their surroundings, children gain firsthand experiences that are built upon their needs and interests. Through the use of their senses and their bodies, children come to understand their environment, themselves, and others. Good planning allows ample opportunities for children to sample experiences and materials that are suitable for their age and developmental level.

In an unpressured way, children are encouraged to express themselves, strengthen their sentence structure, and increase their vocabulary. They should have enough opportunities to talk to themselves, with each other, and with adults. This occurs informally throughout the day as children express what they see around them and match what they see with earlier experiences. Through the child's spontaneous verbal expressions, the adult gains an insight into the child's way of thinking and expressing his emotions.

Children develop their language in the nursery by listening to adults who have good speech patterns and who use simple but exciting language. They can also experiment with language, copy sounds, and discover funny sounds that they enjoy repeating. Their language can also be developed by listening to stories, telling tall tales, making up stories in relation to pictures and picture books, and by listening to songs, nursery rhymes, poems, and folk songs.

Practicing Simple Everyday Activities. The program should allow the child opportunities to practice autonomy in everyday experiences. At this age, children are highly motivated and interested in mastering different activities by themselves.

Conditions should allow for this autonomous growth, the child's developmental stage being taken into consideration. Through play, cleaning up, putting things away, setting the table, etc., a sense of responsibility is acquired. At the same time, the child develops confidence in performing these tasks.

Programs for Children Three to Five Years and Five to Seven Years, or Three to Seven Years Old

In planning these programs, one should understand the children's diverse educational backgrounds. Some come from a sheltered home situation, others have spent time in a supervised play park, while others have attended day care centers. The children's developmental levels and their individual backgrounds should be considered in order that the child has the best conditions possible for growth.

The educational program should include the following:
1. practice of motor abilities and the provision of opportunities for the child to express and release his emotions;

2. stimulating social contact with adults and peers;
3. opportunities for the development of bodily independence of self-care;
4. stimulating constructive play, experimentation, and creative activities;
5. practice in language development and concept formation;
6. fantasies, imaginative and dramatic play, and exercise of practical, ethetical, and musical abilities; and
7. intellectual development and orientation in the immediate surroundings.

In this program, great importance is put upon free group play, and the children are acquainted with the various materials. Immediate involvement is the object, not the attainment of some external goal. Setting such a goal and trying to reach a required standard and produce certain results are not compatible with the child's development. According to the Norwegian point of view, an external goal is not needed to stimulate activities.

Motor Activities. There are opportunities for activities indoors as well as outdoors.

Indoor activities. These include jumping, dancing, balancing, pushing, lifting, rolling, creeping, and sliding. Fine muscle activities are also included such as threading, buttoning, painting, molding, cutting, etc.

Outdoor activities. They are numerous: climbing, swinging, riding a tricycle, kicking, throwing, running, digging, skiing, and sledding.

Some movements and activities are practiced individually or in groups. These activities should give children a chance to move freely, without excessive adult restrictions.

Social Activities. The teacher of this age group influences the child both directly and indirectly. Indirect influence comes through the type of environment she creates, the arrangement of equipment in the playrooms, and the provision of materials. Direct influence comes through her personality and the educational techniques she uses. Her attitude toward a particular child plays a major part in influencing the attitudes of other children toward that child. The teacher's interpretation of acceptable and unacceptable behavior is usually embraced by the children. Each child should feel that he is accepted for what he is and that he belongs to the group.

The teacher organizes conditions in such a way that the child's needs for confidence and social contact will be satisfied through individual and group activities. By allowing free group formation, children get an opportunity to form and dissolve groups. Children establish positive relationships with each other through movement play, sharing time together at meals, and during rest periods.

Each child needs to learn different social techniques; thus, situations should be individualized so as to allow maximum possibilities for individual growth. Aggressive tendencies should be analyzed, and children showing signs of shyness or isolation should be given opportunities for having better social contact.

It is important for older children to gradually learn, through play and other activities, rules necessary for group activities. They should be able to accept their own emotions as well as others, be considerate, and understand how resistance may be met, and to share with others. They also have to learn to take turns and accept responsibility and understand that freedom to carry on their own tasks also implies respect for authority and the rights of others.

Though social activities form a natural part of the educational program through play, it is important that these activities be well-planned.

Intellectual Activities. Young children in the group explore their surroundings as a result of their spontaneous interests. They use their senses and their now improved body control. If the facilities are well structured, the children will obtain a variety of knowledge about themselves, their bodies, and their relationships with materials.

Driven by their own curiosity, children use inductive and deductive reasoning. They generalize from their various experiences and then move from these generalizations to the specific.

Children need many opportunities whereby they may stimulate their concept formation and interest in problem solving. This can be done through observing, comparing, finding similarities and differences, experimenting, analyzing, and organizing and communicating their experiences to other children and adults.

Older children like to determine relationships between an object and its name, an object and its characteristics, reason and effect, etc. The ability to accomplish something new and to discover something for themselves gives children a feeling of self-reliance and self-respect. Their intellectual activities at this stage are based more on emotional and egocentric thinking than on logic and rational coherence.

Children should be given opportunities to experience pleasure through the mastering of problems, and they should feel a joy in learning. This could very well form the basis for a questioning attitude, creative thinking, and effective problem solving. This will result in the child obtaining a feeling of autonomy, emotional stability, and confidence.

Language Stimulation. The aim here would be to increase the child's ability to express himself verbally and enlarge his vocabulary. This can be brought about by imitating a teacher who is a good speech model and through conversations in different sized groups. Different topics relative to their surroundings may be discussed.

Motor play and constructive play will stimulate language in a natural way. Story-telling, listening to stories, singing, etc. also stimulate language development. Other means of stimulation are verbal problem solving, discussions, relating experiences acquired on field trips, nature walks, and everyday living.

Practicing Simple Everyday Experiences. As in the programs for the younger age groups, children in this group are given opportunities to practice their autonomy daily. Through play and participating in tasks such as putting things away, setting the table, and serving, a sense of responsibility may be acquired. An added result would be that the child will feel self-confidence when doing these jobs.

PHYSICAL FACILITIES AND MATERIALS

In a day-care center where children stay for more than six hours a day, the gross area size of a classroom has to be eight square meters for every child over three years old, and twelve square meters for every child under three years of age. The gross land area is fifty square meters per child, parking area and driveway included. The outdoor play space has to be twenty-five square meters per child.

Children who spend most of the day in a care center should be involved in many activities such as indoor and outdoor play, dressing and undressing, washing, using the toilet, preparing meals, eating, and sleeping and resting. The child should not be inactive for long periods of time.

Regular day-care centers are usually housed in independent units built for this purpose. Parent-operated groups may be housed in a private home, a school building, a church or in a community house. The requirements for play area size in this case are three square meters for children aged three to seven and four square meters of play space for children younger than three years. The activities that take place in these groups should preferably be the same as those in regular day-care centers. It is advisable for each group to occupy two rooms or have one room with flexible equipment.

Equipment and Supplies for the Age Group Four Months to One and a Half Years

- Cribs with high sides, one to be lowered.
- Polyfoam mattresses, covers, "dyner" pillows, sheets, "dyner covers," and pillowcases.
- Low tables, low armchairs for the children.
- Tables and chairs for adults.
- Dressing table with polyfoam mattress on top.
- Low shelves for toys and play materials.
- Outdoor cribs with solid sides, outdoor bedding.
- Playpens, highchairs, which can be lowered, infant-seat, baby jump.
- Children's towels, washcloths in two colors, bibs. Adult towels.
- Children's picture identification tag. Lockers for adults.
- First aid cabinet with lock.
- Plastic covered baskets for children to be used in the cloakroom.

Educational Material

For listening: Objects hung out of reach, colored tissue-paper, leaves, etc. Free-hanging wind chimes, wooden rods, bamboo rods, etc. Music box, squeaky rubber animals, sounding blocks made of plastic and wood.

For looking: Bright colored objects within reach: beads, cotton reels, rings. Objects hung out of reach: balloons, colored ribbons, bundles of yarn, windmills, mobiles.

To taste and smell and to shake: Different kinds of rattles, wooden, plastic.

To grasp: Objects right above the crib, plastic animals, soft washable teddybear or rag bag doll.

To throw: Cloth or rubber ball in one solid color.

To manipulate: Small nesting toys.

From One Year Onwards

For Climbing: A movable staircase that can be turned over to be used as a seesaw.

Push toys: Wooden boxes or drawers on rollers. Small stools with handles and rollers to be turned. Wooden doll carriages, beads, empty cans, plastic cars.

To float: Plastic animals.

To push/pull: Animals or objects making music, on rollers with a long string.

To build with: Small cubes in different colors.

To bang: Wooden peg board and hammer.

To nest, take apart, and poke into: Ring-rod, nest of wooden boxes, and other nesting toys. Cars with removable wooden figures.

Beginning imitative household play: Doll with washable cover, teddybears, telephone, cups and saucers made of soft plastic, hats, caps, small handbags, baskets, blankets.

Picture materials: Large clear pictures from the child's world.

Equipment and Supplies for Children One and a Half to Three Years

— Aluminum cots with washable canvas and bedding.
— As in the infant nursery; low tables, chairs and adult chairs and tables. Towels, washcloths, bibs, adult towels.
— Large doll with large bed and bedding.
— Serving table on wheels, wooden shelves for toys and play material.

- Stable wooden screen with a window for the housekeeping corner.
- Flower vases, flower boxes, cosy lamps (on the wall).
- Low slide for indoor use. Easel for painting.
- Large blackboard. Wooden boxes of different sizes on rollers for storage.
- Dressing tables, potties in addition to the small toilets for this group.
- Plastic covered baskets, one for each child's clean diapers brought from home.

Educational material

To slide, push, roll: sawhorse and sliding board, wooden boxes, platform trucks, wheelbarrows, wooden beads, trains, cars, buses, wagons, (preferably at least two of each kind).

To throw: rag balls, table-tennis balls, small plastic balls.

To float: empty cans, rubber or plastic animals.

For imitative household play

Housekeeping equipment and materials: large doll, two to three dolls with washable cover, teddybears, chest of drawers, tables and chairs for the doll-corner, wooden stove for housekeeping play. Coffee pot, small aluminum saucepans, wooden ladles, cups and saucers, plates made of soft plastic or aluminum. Telephones, iron, broom, dustpan.

For creative activities, movement play and initiating constructive play

- Large plastic tablecloth to cover the table.
- Clay, plasticene, plaster powder, salt and flour dough, paper-mâché.
- Manila paper. Different kinds of paper and cardboard in different colors.
- White shelf-paper for fingerpainting. Tissue paper in different colors.
- Paint brushes, crayons, chalk, sponge.
- Powder paint, powder paste, Scotch® tape, string, stapler, cloth-pegs or easer-clips.
- Cloth, felt, yarn, leather, and fur odds and ends.

— Colored icicle sticks. Colored plastic string.

— Shells, shell homes, wooden mosaic, wooden sticks in all colors, feathers.

— Simple kinds of waste materials: boxes, cartons, cotton reels, film reels, cork.

— Large colored beads to put on plastic strings.

For the dress-up corner

— Basket or a wooden box on rollers for dress-up clothes, preferably hats and caps, pieces of clothing, light blankets, cardboard crowns, firemen's helmets, pocketbooks.

For the music corner

— Piano, record player or tape recorder. Music instruments such as tympani sticks, maracas, tambourines, wooden drums, bells on sticks, rattling cans (empty cans with peas inside, can top painted, tightly on).

Noneducational Material

Homemaking equipment: Mugs and small plates for all children and adults, knives, dessert-spoons, a few forks, serving dishes. Bread knives, vegetable knives, coffee pot, tea kettle, tea pot, two saucepans, a small frying pan.

Groceries: sugar, flour, salt, cocoa, instant chocolate and almond pudding, vanilla and raspberry sauce, instant vegetable and meat soups.

Dish pan and dish brush, bench cloth, dust cloth. Floor pail, longhandled mop and floor cloth. Dust pan and short handled broom, longhandled broom. Rolls of paper towels, wax paper, aluminum foil. Paper napkins, tissues.

Equipment and Supplies for Children Three to Five Years, Five to Seven Years, or Three to Seven Years

— Polyfoam pads, two inch thick with zip-off cover for naps, one for each child.

— Blankets with cotton cover.

— Low tables and chairs. Serving table on rollers. Wooden shelves for toys.

— Book rack with slanting shelves. One bench and a large table for book corner.
— Two cabinets with drawers, one for each child.
— Movable trays for children's art work in a cabinet.
— Children's towels, towels for adult use.
— Stable, wooden screen with a window for the doll corner.
— Flower table or flower boxes, wall lamps for doll corner and book corner.
— Bulletin board. Children's picture identification tags.
— Plastic baskets for storing lunch boxes, etc.
— Climbing wall. Woodwork bench or woodwork table.
— Easels, blackboard, sand and water table. Wooden boxes of different sizes for storing material.
— Storage cabinet preferably with movable trays.
— Adult writing table with lockable drawer. Some adult chairs.
— Lockers, one for each adult for personal belongings.
— First aid cabinet with lock.
— Clothes rack for visitors.

Educational Equipment

For motor play: Wheelbarrows, tricycles, trucks, carts, balls, rocking horse, doll carriage, scooter, jungle-gym with slide, rope ladder, manila jump rope, rings, trapeze, tire swings placed horizontally, wooden boxes, boards, saw horses, barrels, ladders, car tires or scooter tires. Plastic snow shuffles and snow shovels, long-handled snow plow.

For dramatic, social, and imitative play: Equipment and supplies for the housekeeping corner such as dolls, doll clothes, chest of drawers, large doll's bed with bedding. Large doll stove made of wood with knobs attached, for the younger child. For the older, an electric stove or stove top with oven, kitchen supplies, toy telephone, or discarded telephone. Store with supplies, lots of scrap materials and wooden box as counter. Balance scales. Pail, long-handled broom, longhandled mop and floor cloth. Dress up chest for dress up clothes, caps, handbags, hats, purses, etc. Hand puppets.

For creative activities and constructive play

— Large plastic table cloth to cover the table.
— Clay, plasticene, plaster powder, mortar powder, salt and flour dough, paper-mâché.
— Manila paper and butcher paper. A wide variety of paper and cardboard in different colors and in white and black silver and gold, crepe paper, tissue paper, white shelf paper for finger painting.
— Paint brushes, longhandled with sturdy bristles.
— Paste brushes, crayons, chalk, sponges, powder paint.
— Blunt scissors, paste, Scotch tape, string, stapler, hole puncher, clothes pegs.
— Trays, picture loops, button forms (wooden).
— Small looms, weaving needles, odds and ends of cloth, felt, yarn, leather, fur, beads, textile glue.
— Plastic string, colored pipe cleaners, sucking straws, shells, empty snail shells, glass and rock mosaic shapes, wooden sticks in a variety of colors, feathers, Styrofoam balls, flower wire
— A large variety of waste materials (boxes, cartons, empty cotton reels, film reels, empty match boxes, cork).
— Plenty of solid unit blocks, large and small ones.
— Connector, Lego, Belofix, Brio construction sets.

For the music corner

— Piano, record player, or tape recorder.
— Simple Orff instruments and other rhythm instruments such as tambourines, triangles, sticks and castanettes. Wooden drums (tom-tom, bongo, Indian), bells.
— Music boxes, song books and books about singing games and rhythmical games.

For the library corner

— Pictures, picture books and reference books about animals, plants, the body, and planets, climatic conditions, and transportation.
— Games for developing concentration, lotto games, puzzles, racing games such as ludo, ladder games, road safety games.

For simple woodwork

- Tools (adult quality), smallest size of hammer, screw driver, bit auger, gimlet, files, pliers, saws of different sizes, yard stick, band paper, nails, screws, carpenter glue, ruler.
- Soft wood and mill scraps of pine and fir, odds of plywood, cotton reels, etc.

Equipment for the outdoor play area

- Sand box or sand pit, sturdy tables and benches.
- Two swings with horizontally placed tires, a small jungle-gym with a slide attached.
- Rope ladder, playhouse.
- Manila climbing rope with knobs, gym rings.

All of these should be placed on a sandy surface so as to avoid injury if the children happen to fall.

Additional equipment and supplies that would also be very useful are:

- Several wine barrels, which can be remodeled for use as an airplane, train, etc.
- An enclosed space made up of crated, wooden boxes, boards, ladders and solid unit blocks.
- Wheelbarrows, large trucks, tricycles, shovels (small and junior sizes).
- Tins and pails, plastic snow shovels.

Meals in Day-Care Centers

In day-care centers operating from 8 a.m. to 5 p.m., a hot meal is served in addition to the Oslo-breakfast which consists of whole wheat bread, hard bread, butter, cheese, liver paste, milk, fruit, and cod-liver-oil. The Oslo-breakfast is sometimes served in schools or setups in which children bring their own sandwiches and are supplied with mild fruit and cod-liver-oil by the personnel. There are no state laws regarding the nutritional consciousness, but proper nourishment is offered in these schools.

STRENGTHS AND WEAKNESSES OF THESE PROGRAMS

The primary strength of these programs is the fact that children are allowed to be children until they are seven. No one forces them to read and write before they actually start elementary school.

Another strength is the law for *barnehager*. These guidelines can be followed when building *barnehager* all over the country, taking into account the local needs of the communities. A certain uniformity exists, be it a day-care center open nine hours a day, a teacher- or parent-operated group open for as little as six hours a week, or a family day-care center setup. Another positive factor is that provision is made for the integration of handicapped children into the regular programs.

The main weakness of these programs relates to the handicapped. With their integration, the need for more personnel arises. Often an additional person is added for this purpose. The regular groups are already so large that it is not possible to give enough attention to the needs of the handicapped. The future goal is to cut down on the size of the groups so that the handicapped children who are integrated can receive more attention.

SUMMARY

This chapter has discussed the organization and operation of *Barnehager* or preschool programs in Norway.

The centers that operate these programs are divided into different age groups, i.e. four months to one-and-a-half years, one-and-a-half to three years, three to five, and five to seven. The main objectives of these programs are

1. to provide a favorable environment in which play is emphasized and interaction is encouraged;
2. to provide guidance in the development of the child's personality; and
3. to structure activities which are compatible with the child's developmental level.

The *Barnehager* are controlled by the ministry of Consumers and Administration, which establishes rules and regulations that need to be followed. Each county has a supervisor who sees to it that these programs are properly run, and on the local level an Early Childhood Committee plans, builds, and operates the early childhood programs in the community.

The ministry subsidizes early childhood programs with the communities and the individual parents contributing towards the operating costs. Regarding tuition, a nominal fee is paid with children of needy families attending free of charge.

Physical plant and facilities are more than adequate. The main emphasis of the curriculum is on free-play periods that encourages self-awareness, language and intellectual development, the acquisition of basic skills, and the development of a good self-concept.

In these programs, children are allowed to remain children for as long as possible, which is important for their future development.

REFERENCES

Lov om 'Barnehager' med forskrifter og Kommentarer, Fosbrukerog Administrasjonsdepartementet, Familie-og Forbrukeravdelingin (no printing date). Translation: *Law for 'Barnehager,'* with regulations and comments, Ministry for Consumers and Administration, Family and Consumers Department.

"Barnehagens mal og innhold," en seminarrapport, juni 1981. Norsk Omep. (Barnehage, It objectives and rationale) Report from a conference.

Berg, Turi Sverdrup: "Mannlige studenter og forskolelaerere i studium og yrkesliv." Hosten 1980. (Male students and teachers of young children during studies and work) Fall 1980.

"Familiebarnehagen." Juni 1981. Report from a conference for teachers as leaders for a group of family day care parents. June 1981. FAD. Forbruker- og administrasjonsdepartementet, Familie-og likestillingsavdelingen

Bleken, Unni: "Oppfolging av barnehager fir fremmedspraklige barn." Mai 1981. Report from a project: Follow-up-studies of barnehager for XXX bilingual children, May 1981. FAD. Forbruker- og administrasjonsdepartmentet, Familie-og likestillingsavdelingen.

Chapter 11

EARLY CHILDHOOD SERVICES
IN ALBERTA, CANADA

GEETA R. LALL and BERNARD M. LALL

INTRODUCTION

I N March 1973, the government of Alberta established the
Early Childhood Services Branch in the Department of Education. Initially it worked formally with the other departments
of Advanced Education, Culture, Health and Social Development
and Youth Recreation. As of November 1982, it works formally
with Advanced Education and Community Health and Social
Services. Early Childhood Services (E.C.S.) coordinates the services provided by these departments, other departments, and
agencies in helping meet the needs of young children and their
families. Programs are offered for children, parents, staff, and
community.

PHILOSOPHY

The central purpose of E.C.S. is to strengthen the sense of
dignity and the self-worth within a child by providing a combined
effort of the family, the staff, and the community in the overall
development of a child's activities. During the child's formative
years, physical, intellectual, and social qualities are being developed. These are all related and depend on each other. Once these

The authors wish to thank E.A. Torgunrud, Director of Early Childhood Services,
Alberta, Canada, for his help in compiling some of the materials provided in this chapter.

needs are met, the child is more likely to have the ability to interact with others, to judge and control responses, and to follow
directions: he also develops self-reliance, initiative, and respect
for the rights of others and experiences the stimulation of aesthetic awareness.

An individual's self-concept is dependent, to a large extent,
on the ability to think logically and to express these thoughts in
an intelligent manner. Thus, the development of the elements of
thinking and the components of language formation are dependent
on programs directed by a staff that possesses the knowledge, the
necessary skills, and a variety of background training to meet the
needs of young children.

The development of motor skills and the senses helps the child
become aware of his body's capabilities. His sensory development
helps him to evaluate his environment. The child's experiences,
acquaintances, and view of life should constantly be broadened
in order that all interest and need areas may be covered.

The environment plays an important part in the child's personal development. The commitment of parents and others to
share the responsibility in the implementation of programs to
meet the developmental needs of the child, enhances the dignity
and worth of the family as a fundamental unit in society. Physical, cognitive, and emotional factors must be considered within
the home environment.

Health, educational, social, emotional, and physical needs
require an approach that extends beyond the school experiences.
Programs should be flexible to meet the cultural and economical
standards and the geographical location of a community. The delivery of services should be comprehensive enough to provide
room for allowing voluntary decisions on enrollment age, for
assisting in the enrollment for children with special needs, and for
providing resource persons to assist in meeting the needs of children and their families and the community at large.

OBJECTIVES OF EARLY CHILDHOOD SERVICES

The objectives of E.C.S. are as follows:
1. Looking after the physical, dental, and nutritional needs and
   demands of children

2. Strengthening the child's social and emotional development

3. Providing stimulating activities to strengthen mental skills and processes

4. Providing success experiences, thus promoting self-confidence

5. Permitting the child to interact with his family, peers, and community

6. Developing a responsible attitude toward society, along with individual and group cooperation in the solution of problems

Basic Principles of E.C.S.

1. The E.C.S. must provide the conditions necessary for change. It should include everyone from the child, parent, teacher, and recreational leaders to psychologists.

2. E.C.S. must facilitate feedback. Each division of E.C.S. must know what effect it is having on young children.

3. E.C.S. must support a high degree of diversity. This is brought about if services are offered by a variety of agencies in various locations.

4. E.C.S. must seek to avoid overlapping of services.

5. E.C.S. must compromise the forces of integration and decentralization. Various agencies may assume the responsibility for the development of young children.

6. E.C.S. must provide for planned development but allow for uneven growth.

Basic Goals of E.C.S.

1. To provide adequate health care, and the development of gross motor, fine motor, and perceptual motor skills

2. To enhance the development of social skills

3. To develop a positive self-concept in young children

4. To contribute to the intellectual growth of young children

5. To stimulate creativity by the use of past and present experiences and the expression of self through the arts

6. To involve parents in the E.C.S. program

7. To provide professional growth for the staff

8. To contribute to a comprehensive system of early childhood services, which will provide opportunities for individuals, families, and communities to work together in meeting
the needs of young children.

ORGANIZATION AND ADMINISTRATION OF E.C.S.

The Department of Advanced Education, Education and Social Services, and Community Health are jointly responsible for
Early Childhood Services. While working jointly these departments still maintain their independence. The coordinated approach works as follows:

Provincial

An Early Childhood Services Policy Advisory Council of thirteen members has representation from universities, colleges, E.C.S.
centers, health units, regional coordinating committees, parents,
and public at large. It has a nonvoting representative from each of
the participating departments. The council advises the deputy
ministers of the respective departments and through them the
ministers of the departments. The ministers in turn report to
government through the cabinet (departmental ministers) and the
legislature. The council meets four times a year and advises upon
policy and guidelines for Early Childhood Services. Informal relationships with departments other than the preceding are maintained for coordinating government programs directed at the parent, child, and the community groups.

Within the policy and guidelines approved by government, the
operational planning, program development, and approval and development of program resources is done. A director of the E.C.S.
branch, responsible for the services, reports to the Assistant Deputy Minister, Program Development. Branch staff E.C.S. consultants, located in five regional offices throughout the province,
assist center operators and parents in the conduct of E.C.S. programs.

Doctors and nurses in health units, social workers in regional
offices, and other field personnel from other departments, also
assist.

Local

On the local level, E.C.S. services are operated by a school or incorporated nonprofit societies. A Local Advisory Committee (L.A.C.) advises the operator on all matters.

The functions of the L.A.C. may include assistance in staff selection, parent-child development programs, and opening toy and book-lending centers.

Local Advisory Committees provide a means for parents to contribute to the E.C.S. program in their community and keep in touch with what is happening. L.A.C. also acquaints parents with program specifics and the ways they relate to the needs of children and parents in their community.

The E.C.S. programs consist of four separate but interrelated areas: children's programs, parents' programs, staff programs, and community programs.

Children's programs may operate in centers where the child attends a given number of half days or full days per week. In-home programs without official licensing as instructional settings are limited in enrollment to three children, and the parents are assisted by teachers who make regular visits to the home. Another option for children's programs is a combination of center and in-home programs. The program could operate in a center two half-days per week, and the balance of the program would consist of home visits.

Parents' programs provide study groups or workshops related to child development and child-rearing practices. Parents are also given the opportunity to work as aids in their children's programs.

Staff visit other E.C.S. programs and attend university courses and developmental workshops, and the community programs provide information about services offered, involve high-school work-experience students in programs for young children, and provide further education courses about parenting and family living.

The E.C.S. programs for children are broken down into three categories: Category A — programs for children who are handicapped, Category B — programs for disadvantaged children, and Category C — programs for children who have normal needs.

Handicapped Children — Category A

Category A children can enroll in E.C.S. if they are three and one-half years old on September 1 of the school year. The program offered to them is remedial and/or adaptive in nature and selective in scope. In the cases of hearing impaired children and severely (profoundly) handicapped children, the E.C.S. program is available to them if they are two and one-half years old as of September 1.

Disadvantaged Children — Category B

Children in category B are culturally different and/or educationally disadvantaged. They must be four and one-half years old on September 1 of the school year to qualify. Their programs may be compensatory, preventive, and enriching in nature but selective in scope.

Normal Children — Category C

Children considered normal must be four and one-half years old on September 1 of the school year to qualify.

FINANCES

Revenue for preschoolers is obtained from provincial grants and is contingent upon 400 hours of program offered on a half-day basis. Approved E.C.S. programs that operate less than 400 hours are eligible for a prorated grant.

For each handicapped child, the school district or other operating body received a per-pupil grant, the amount depending upon the type of handicap. For example, grants for different handicaps are paid according to the following schedule (1983):

Category	Per Pupil Grant (based on 400 hours of attendance)
Mentally retarded, visually impaired, learning disabled child	$1,860
Hearing handicapped, emotionally disturbed	2,250
Physically handicapped	2,025
Dependent handicapped or multiple-handicapped children in program unit	1,820*

---

*plus grants ranging from $21,800 to $43,600 depending on the number of students enrolled, which in turn range from one to seven or more in an instructional unit.

The grants for these categories are larger than those for other children because of the specialized and individualized nature of the program components.

Grants for disadvantaged children are equivalent to 75 percent of the full-time per-child grant for elementary-school pupils. In 1983, this amounted to $1,290 per child. The grants are greater to meet the additional services required by children in this category.

Programs offered for normal children receive a per-child grant that is equal to 60 percent of that for elementary-school pupils, $1,676. Grants for handicapped or disadvantaged children who attend normal preschools are based on the same schedules as those in schools for the handicapped and disadvantaged. Funding is also available for the preadmission assessment of handicapped children, $185 per child.

Grants paid to private agencies serving handicapped children are equal to those paid public or separate schools providing these programs meet E.C.S. guidelines.

Transportation grants are provided for all handicapped children and for certain other students in rural communities or second-language classes. The grant amounts are as follows:

1. Transportation of handicapped children in rural and urban areas — $7.20
2. Transportation of eligible regular children in urban areas — $2.00
3. Transportation of eligible children in rural areas — $2.10

E.C.S. CURRICULUM

The objectives and emphases of E.C.S. programs should grow out of the needs of the children. The following areas are considered in the programs:

— Health and physical development
— Social development
— Emotional and affective development
— Self-concept development
— Intellectual development
— Creative development

— Parent involvement
— Staff development and community services

Indoor Activities

1. Household play — gives children an opportunity to experience household activities.
2. Art — gives children the chance to express thoughts, feelings, dreams, and visions creatively.
3. Music — provides opportunities for creative expression, aids in the development of listening, and coordinates skills.
4. Dramatic play — aids in language development, manipulative skills, development of concepts, sensory awareness, and ideas for music and art. It also provides opportunities for creative expression.
5. Block play — aids development in areas such as intellectual growth, perceptual development, motor development, and problem-solving skills. This can be used with individuals or small groups of children.
6. Manipulative play with materials — aids the development of visual discrimination, eye-hand coordination, memory, matching, and classifying.
7. Movement experiences — serve to aid development of thinking and problem-solving skills, creativity, large and small muscle coordination, and strength.
8. Food preparation — aids development of gross and fine motor skills, following sequential directions, counting, measuring, classifying skills, and understanding principles of nutrition.
9. Woodwork and carpentry — aid development of gross and fine motor control, perceptual awareness, problem solving, and language.
10. Sand and water play — aid development of language concepts, creativity, socialization, mathematical and scientific concepts, motor development, and problem solving.
11. Mathematics — aids development of understanding in sorting and classifying, counting, measurement, volume, and shape.
12. Science — aids development of ability to actively process information received through the senses.

13. Language — aids development of listening, viewing, reading, writing, and speaking skills for immediate and/or future use.

Outdoor Activities

Children need opportunities to enjoy and experience the outdoors and the things it has to offer. The need to jump, skip, hop, feel the grass against their skin, and observe insects and small animals with all the freedom that can be offered. All these activities help them to develop physically, mentally, and emotionally. These may be developed through some of the following elements:

1. A hill — can be made from dirt and used for toboggans, sleds, and homemade go-carts. The other side of the hill could be used as a slide. Play in this area is very safe.
2. Sand — is a manipulative, creative substance. It should be deep enough for making castles, and equipment such as pails, sieves, and spoons should be available.
3. Water — is very valuable from the developmental standpoint. Without it, sand loses much of its value. Children could make streams, dams, sailboats, etc.
4. Swings — contribute to physical development and often serve as an emotional retreat and consoler.
5. Climbing apparatus — includes jungle gyms. These present excellent challenges and are useful in adding imaginative play.
6. Playhouses — encourage social play, stimulate the imagination, and invite verbal interaction.
7. Blocks — serve as an excellent medium of creative play.
8. Gardening — is conducive to learning and to emotional satisfaction.
9. Animals — provide children with an opportunity to learn about living things; the care and feeding of animals is an important part of a child's development.
10. Group activity area — provides opportunities for socialization.
11. Wheel toy area — provides a hard, smooth path or roadway where trucks, wagons, etc. can be used. Children could learn rules of traffic in this area.
12. Quite place — provides children with a rest area away from other activities.

13. A natural area — has grass, trees, flowers, bugs, etc. The possibilities for experiences in this area are endless.

FACILITIES

Typical E.C.S. centers may include the following:
- Open area for large group activity
- Quiet area for individual activity
- Book or library center
- Assembly center
- Housekeeping area
- Art center
- Math center
- Science center
- Water center
- Food-preparation center
- Woodwork and carpentry center
- Music center
- Construction center

Rooms should have a flexible arrangement: equipment and material most often used together are placed in proximity. Children should have clear pathways through the room. The arrangement of materials and equipment should be such as to encourage independent use, cleanup, and storage by the children. The room should also be arranged to allow staff to supervise and interact with the children with maximum effectiveness.

MATERIALS

Materials are listed under the headings used in the previous section.

Indoor Materials

1. Furniture — tables, chairs, lockers; all child size and safe for children's use.
2. Art — large pencils, crayons, wax, chalk, paper of all kinds, paint, brushes, sponges, easels, smocks, clay, plasticene, boxes, adhesives, scissors, etc.
3. Music — record player, records, instruments such as piano,

Autoharp, xylophone, guitar, drums, tambourine, triangle, sand blocks, etc.

4. Dramatic play — child-size furnishings, telephone, mirrors, cooking utensils, flashlights, ropes, binoculars, combs, brushes, wigs, etc.
5. Block play — solid unit blocks, solid table blocks, hollow large block.
6. Manipulative materials — puzzles, beads, pegboards, lotto games, pounding sets, typewriters, card games, etc.
7. Movement experiences — jungle-gym, ladders, stairs, trees, large barrels, pipes, benches, tunnels, mats, tricycle, bicycle, walking boards, bean bags, balls, boxes, etc.
8. Food preparation — hot plate, frying pan, blender, refrigerator, oven, mixing and eating utensils, foodstuffs, etc.
9. Woodwork and carpentry — tools scrap wood, nails, tacks, sandpaper, screws, hooks, etc.
10. Sand and water play — sand table, sand, shovels, buckets, funnels, large basin, objects that sink or float, etc.
11. Mathematics — shells, buttons, beads, mosaic shapes, nails, blocks, paint, tongue depressors, dominoes, etc.
12. Science — colors, living plants, rocks, animals, wood pieces, leaves, tree bark, different kinds of nails and screws, spices, fruits, perfumes, sandpaper, sound-making materials, etc.
13. Language — record and tape player, radio, television, slide and filmstrip projector, picture books, puppets, paintings, dress-up clothes, flannel board, book-display area, rug, pillows, stuffed chairs, etc.

Outdoor Materials

1. Sand, toboggans, sleds, slides
2. Sand play — pails, sieves, spoons, etc.
3. Water play — pails, cups, spoons, boats, wood, etc.
4. Swings
5. Climbing apparatus — jungle gyms, knotted ropes, fireman's poles, ropes, trapezes, ladders, bridges, pulley rides, etc.
6. Playhouses — miniature cottages, tree houses, caves, nooks, teepees, grocery store, post office, etc.
7. Blocks

8. Loose materials — wooden boxes of different sizes, boards, small ladders, sawhorses, solid or hollow blocks, loose wood —in different sizes, old tires, pots and pans, dress-up clothes, old washtubs, etc.

9. Animals — birds, fish, rabbits, goats, hamsters, etc.

10. Wheel toy area — wagons, tricycle, stop signs, gas station, garage, parking area, etc.

STAFF

For handicapped children, a certified teacher is required, regardless of the size of the group. The number of aides and assistants depends on the type and severity of the handicap. The staff/child ratio is lower than for normal children. For disadvantaged children, the ratio is 1:18, and for normal children the recommended ratio is 1:22.

Teachers must be certified and hold an Alberta Teaching Certificate with a major in Early Childhood Education and an Early Childhood Services Diploma. In addition to the teacher, other specialized instructional assistants and aides may be required in order to provide a full complement of social, health, and educational services.

SUMMARY

The major long-range goal of E.C.S. is the strengthening of the child's dignity and self-worth. This can be done by taking care of the educational, health, family, and social needs.

The E.C.S. program standards are set on the provincial level, but local discretion and initiatives may be exercised. Early-childhood consultants are provided by the Department of Education to assist local authorities in any way necessary.

The curriculum is flexible and places much emphasis on play activities. Facilities are arranged and constructed in line with the program objectives.

Grants are provided on the basis of programs operating 400 hours on a half-day basis. The amounts given for handicapped programs are much higher than those for other programs because of the specialized services and facilities that are used. Program-unit grants for severely handicapped children permit an operator to offer 800 or more hours of programs in a center or a home-based program comprised of a minimum of thirty-six home visits.

Teachers must have a degree in Early Childhood Education and must be certified by the province of Alberta. The teacher/ child ratio is recommended at a level of 1:18 for disadvantaged children, 1:22 for normal children. The teacher/handicapped children ratio is considerably lower and is determined by the severity of the handicap.

The E.C.S. programs endeavor to involve parents and local communities and try to use existing physical and human resources to the greatest possible extent.

REFERENCES

Alberta Early Childhood Services. *Community Services/Resource Guide.* September 1980.

– – – . *Helping Children Learn through Field Experience: A Guide to Parents.* Edmonton.

– – – . *How to Evaluate Your E.C.S. Program.* Edmonton.

– – – . *Self-Evaluation: A Handbook for E.C.S. Staff.* Edmonton.

– – – . *Operating an E.C.S. Program: An Administrative Handbook.* Edmonton, 1981.

Alberta Educational Communications Corporation. *Focus on Childhood.* Edmonton, 1977.

Early Childhood Services: Philosophy, Goals and Program Dimensions, interim edition. Alberta, Canada, 1982.

Chapter 12

COMPARISON OF EARLY CHILDHOOD
EDUCATION PROGRAMS

BERNARD M. LALL, GEETA R. LALL,

and MAURICE DUPREEZ

IN the preceding chapters, the reader has hopefully obtained an overview of all preschool education in countries we dealt with. In the course of reading, differences and similarities have been noted, and that was the whole purpose of this volume.

This chapter will compare various aspects of preschool educational programs under individual subheadings. Before doing that, however, a brief summary of each country will be given, in order to refresh the reader's mind and allow him to better make a comparative judgement.

U.S.S.R.

Early childhood education in the Soviet Union emphasizes precocity. This is based on the belief that 90 percent of the child's upbringing is completed by the time he is five years old. Since he eventually will have to master certain developmental and educational skills, he may as well start work on these areas as early in life as possible.

Preschools are important in this nation where 80 percent of the women work. They are not a recent innovation, the first Directorate of Preschool Education having been established shortly after the Revolution of October 1917. This Directorate still administers preschool programs in conjunction with the joint commission of the Academy of Pedagogical Sciences of the Russian Republic and the Academy of Medical Sciences of the Soviet Union.

All preschools have a director, who is usually a woman. The rest of the staff includes teachers, medical personnel, a cook, domestic, and custodial help. Teachers normally have a college degree and have taken courses in child psychology, theories of learning, and other specialty areas, e.g. art, music.

Preschools are provided for all children under seven years of age. In addition to regular preschools, there are boarding schools, forest schools operated for children with health problems, and schools for exceptional children. These schools are all funded by the state. Tuition ranging from thirty to 150 rubles is also charged.

Early Childhood Education programs are divided into six groups, roughly corresponding to the first six years of life. The curriculum normally includes physical and psychological development, social skills, language development, aesthetic appreciation, and environmental orientation. Classes meet in two-story buildings for nurseries and three-story buildings for kindergartens. The grounds are covered with trees and shrubs, and they have sufficient educational materials and playground equipment.

ISRAEL

Jewish preschools were primarily established for the teaching of Jewish knowledge and values—the transmission of their cultural heritage. Programs currently aim at the development of the child's personality and capacities and preparation for participation in life.

The earliest preschools were established by the first Zionist immigrants (1880) for the revival of Hebrew as a modern language. Eventually other subjects were also taught in Hebrew. The first kindergarten was established in 1898, but it wasn't until 1948 that the ministry of Education and Culture was established. A special department within the ministry is responsible for government funded preschool classes.

All teachers in Jewish preschools are women. Arab preschools have 60 percent male teachers. In addition to teachers, there are aides, rhythmics teachers, nurses, support staff, and other professionals who are available as needed. Teachers undergo two to three years of training in colleges or seminaries. Training for teachers in a kibbutz ranges from attendance at three-month seminars to full fledged teachers courses.

In 1976-77, there were 5000 preschool classes with 165,000 children between the ages of three and six. No tuition is charged, the schools being funded by local bodies.

The curriculum in these preschools is predominantly content centered and group oriented, with the emphasis in kibbutz schools being on independent activity and self-expression. Classes meet in specially constructed buildings, usually near an elementary school, with two classes in one building sharing common areas. In the kibbutz, classes meet in the children's houses, which contain facilities for children of a particular age group.

INDIA

The Indian philosophy of Early Childhood Education is based on the belief that preschool education should be available to the masses, not just to the elite class. The influence of Montessori and Froebel is evident, although there is an emphasis on indigenous philosophies.

Most of the preschools were originally private undertakings. Although the Sergeant Committee issued a document on preschool education in 1944, no action was taken on its recommendations. Schools eventually were organized under state regulations and are currently the responsibility of the Director of Social Welfare within the Central Welfare Board.

Staff for preschools consists of a director, teachers, and aides. Depending on their position and responsibilities, teachers undergo two to three month crash courses, eleven month certificate courses, or one year courses.

Preschool programs may include any of the following: Montessori schools, kindergartens, minimum-standard preschools, mobile creches for working mothers, and laboratory preschools attached to universities. The exact number of children serviced has been difficult to ascertain. However in 1974, there were four million children attending preschool programs. These schools are funded by the state and through contributions from the community and foreign programs such as CARE.

The curriculum has been influenced by Montessori. It includes exercises in practical life, education of the senses, intellectual education, muscular education, and language skills. Schools may meet in buildings, under a tree, in an open court yard, or on the verandah of a school. Equipment and materials are adequate.

JAPAN

The Japanese believe that education should begin as early as possible. Preschool programs should develop the intellect, cultivate the mind and body, contribute to the child's social and moral development, and supplement home education.

The first kindergartens were established in 1876, with the first regulations adopted in 1889-1890. These regulations were revamped in 1899 and remained in force until the Kindergarten Act was passed in 1926. Currently, kindergartens are administered by the Ministry of Education.

All kindergartens have a director, along with teachers, nurses, a clerk, dentist, physician, and a pharmacist. The staff for day nurseries consists of day nurses and part-time physicians. Kindergarten teachers have a bachelor's degree or a junior college diploma, while day nursery personnel are graduates of day nursery training institutes.

In 1977, 65.1 percent of five-year-olds attended kindergarten and 25.4 percent attended day nursery. These programs are offered in parks, playgrounds, and children's homes. Funding for kindergartens is provided by the Japanese government for national kindergartens, by local communities for public kindergartens, and through contributions and tuition for private kindergartens. Day nurseries are funded by local communities and through tuition charges.

Programs cover the following areas: health, social studies, nature, language, music and rhythm, drawing, and handicrafts. Classes generally meet in a one-story building and have adequate facilities for education, health, sanitation, administration and play.

CHINA

Chinese educators believe that education in their country has a three-fold purpose: to contribute to the ideological conversion of the Chinese, to contribute to the national economy by using productive physical labor, and to weave education into the life of the masses. Their educational philosophy is based on these principles.

Prior to 1949, the literacy rate in China stood at 20 percent. In 1951, the Government Administration Council issued the "Decisions Concerning Reforms of the Educational System" which became the basis of the national system of education. This led to the establishment of nursery schools in addition to regular schools. Regulations were set by the Central Ministry of Education, which still oversees preschool education today. Individual schools, however, are run by local People's Councils, rural communes, urban factories, offices, industries, and residential areas.

Preschool classes are staffed mainly by housewives and young girls who have undergone very short training courses (as of 1970). This may have changed with the new reform movement that is now sweeping China.

China, as of 1958, had forty-one million nursery school children and had a national literacy rate of 90 percent as compared to 20 percent in pre-1949 years. Programs are funded by the government and through tuition.

Children are taught music, calisthenics, productive labor, language skills, art, and general knowledge. Classes are held in old mansions, individual buildings, or in a few rooms in primary schools. Equipment includes tricycles and building blocks.

ENGLAND

Early Childhood Education originally was a social reform movement. For this reason, priority was given to disadvantaged children.

The decision that a child should start school at five years of age was made over a century ago, not as a result of contemporary research, but in an attempt to ameliorate the wretched social conditions of child labor. Today it is regarded as a privilege to send kids to nursery school.

The responsibility for education is that of the office of the Secretary of State for Education and Science. Nursery schools and classes for children aged three to five are administered by the Department of Education and Science; the Department of Health and Social Security administers day nurseries for children from birth through five years of age.

Nursery schools must be in the charge of a qualified head teacher. At least half of the staff are qualified nursery nurses, not qualified teachers. Support staff includes a social worker. Teachers must have a degree, while nursery nurses undergo two years of training at a college of further education.

Programs are offered in nursery schools and preschool centers. In 1976, only 10 percent of children aged two to five attended 600 nursery schools. Forty-five thousand children went full-time, while 100,000 only went part-time. Financing comes from the government (65%) with the rest contributed by local authorities.

Nursery schools emphasize physical activities, music, poetry, language development, and development of self-reliance, independence, and cooperation. Infant schools concentrate on language development, early scientific and mathematical ideas, physical coordination, and the development of social relationships and aesthetic responses. Classes are held in single story buildings that have a sheltered play area, space for outdoor play and for gardens, a lounge room for parents, furniture, play equipment, etc.

U.S.A.

Preschool education philosophy combines the theories of Piaget and Dewey and those of the British infant school. The child should be helped to better understand himself and his environment. Education deals with the child's social, emotional, cognitive, and motor development.

Although day care has been in existence for over 100 years, it has generally been a private enterprise. The first centers started in the 1850s as social welfare institutions. They served as child care centers during World Wars I and II when mothers had to work.

In 1933, day care was authorized as part of the Works Progress Administration. This responsibility was shifted to the Office of Defense, Health, and Welfare Services in 1942. Day care centers were to have been disbanded when World War II ended, but since many women still worked outside the home, they became a permanent institution. Presently, day care programs are administered by the Community Services Administration of the Health, Education and Welfare. On the local level, each center has a board of directors that exercises direct control over the program.

Personnel includes a director, teachers and aides, a cook, medical personnel, and custodial help. Teachers are trained at a four or two year college with courses relevant to Early Childhood Education included in their programs.

Day care programs may be offered by the following organizations: Family Child Care, Home Play Groups, Parent Cooperative Child Care Programs, Parent and Child and Teacher Program, Child Care Aide Service, and Head Start. These may all fall under those general program types: In-home care (37%), Family day care (47%), and Center care (16%). Funding is provided by federal, state, and local authorities and by private groups, individuals, and parents.

Activities touch on the physical, emotional, and intellectual needs for adequate growth and development. They include music, reading, sand and water play, block-building, games, and domestic skills. Classrooms allow freedom of movement and have different learning centers and materials for different activities.

MEXICO

The emphasis of preschool education is on providing the individual child with educational experiences that stress interaction with the environment and development of skills that enable him to achieve his maximum potential and to control and modify his environment. The development of the individual is a corollary to contributing to the society in which he lives.

Kindergartens first appeared in 1904. The Ministry of Education first entered the picture in 1928. During the next decade, the influence of Soviet educational theory was first felt. As a result of this, kindergartens were removed from the Department of Education and placed under the Department of Public Welfare. Soviet influence ended in 1940, and preschool education was moved back to the Ministry of Education. Programs are currently administered by the office of the General Director of Preschool Education, who is responsible to the Minister of Education of the Federal government.

Preschools have a director, teachers, and other support staff. Teachers have to have a four year degree with an area of specialization such as music, art, etc.

In 1978, Mexico had 1000 preschools, 900 of those situated in Mexico City. Funding is provided by federal and state governments plus tuition charges. Physical plant is provided by the government, while parents supply the equipment.

Health, hygiene, recreation, patriotism, creative arts, family, school, and social awareness are emphasized. Classes are held in single story buildings with adequate facilities for education, health, sanitation, administration, and playing areas.

SWEDEN

Educational philosophy is based on the theories of Gesell, Piaget, and Erikson. There is an emphasis on the child's personal and social development, one complementing the other. An environment is provided that is socially and physically stimulating. In this environment, children, unpressured, will discover their world.

Nursery schools have not been in existence very long. Only in the 1960s were serious ideas formulated to set up such schools. The supreme authority for these schools is the Ministry of Health and Social Affairs. However, the National Board of Health and Welfare does the actual supervision. The County Administration is the regional authority, and on the local level the Child Welfare Committees are in control.

Staff consists of a director, teachers, nurses, kitchen staff, and maintenance workers. Nursery school teachers complete a two year college course, preschool teachers study for two or four years, and day care mothers take a ninety hour course in child care.

Day nurseries cater to children aged six months to seven years, and nursery schools serve children aged three to six years old. Other centers that admit children of preschool age are municipal, family, day nurseries, farming day nurseries, and recreation centers.

Finances are shared among the state (35%), municipality (50%), and parents (15%). Parents pay tuition according to their income level.

The curriculum includes social, emotional, physical, and intellectual development. Other areas taught are self-help skills, fine and gross motor skills, respect for rules and prohibitions, and the ability to communicate effectively with others. Classes are held in one story buildings specially designed for each age group. Facilities include play equipment and learning materials.

NORWAY

Educational philosophy has been influenced by Rousseau, Pestallozi, Froebel, Decroly, Kilpatrick, Montessori, Isaacs, Piaget, and Gesell. Preschool education is basically a nurturing process. The child's need for affection and security have to be met. He also needs to be accepted by peers and grown-ups and, at the same time, gain independence and self-respect.

Prior to 1975, Norwegian preschools were divided into two groups: one catering to children from birth to three years of age and the other from age three to seven. The Barnehager Law of 1975 set forth rules and regulations regarding preschools, grouped them together, and henceforth referred to them as Barnehager. This law put preschools under the control of the Ministry of Consumers and Administration. Each region has a County Supervisor, and on the local level, there are Early Childhood Committees.

Each school has a trained director and teachers, plus support staff, which in many cases are parents. Teachers have to take a teacher course.

Schools can be set up by private individuals, companies, hospitals, church groups, or housewife organizations. Funds are obtained through government subsidies, contributions by communities and parents, and through tuition, which is charged those who can afford it.

Daily programs emphasizing free-play periods encourage self-awareness, language and intellectual development, the acquisition of basic skills, and the development of a good self-concept. Children meet in specially built schools, private homes, classrooms in a regular school building, churches, and community houses. They have ample educational and playground materials.

ALBERTA, CANADA

The central purpose of preschool education is to strengthen the sense of dignity and the self-worth within a child and his parents. Health, educational, social, emotional, and physical needs have to be met in cooperation with the home.

The Early Childhood Services Branch was established by the government of Alberta in March 1973. This branch works closely with the Departments of Health and Social Development, Culture, Youth, and Recreation, Advanced Education, and Education. On the provincial level, the overall administration of Early Childhood Services programs is undertaken by a Coordination Council, chaired by the Associate Deputy Minister of Education. Programs are administered on the local level by schools, private institutions, agencies, individuals, and Early Childhood Services Advisory Committees.

Staff consists of certified teachers, aides, assistants, and other support personnel. The teacher/child ratio varies from 1:8 to 1:22. Teachers all have a college degree with a major in Early Childhood Education.

Early Childhood Services consists of center programs, in-home programs, and a combination of center and in-home programs. Parent programs are also offered and include workshops dealing with child-rearing and developmental practices. Funding comes from provincial grants, which are contingent upon 540 hours of program offered on a half-day basis.

The curriculum includes language skills, acquisition of basic skills, cognitive, emotional, affective, motor, perceptual, and social development, and the development of self-concept. The programs have flexible room arrangements with learning and activity centers set up around the room. Materials are available as required by program objectives.

COMPARISONS

When examining the different programs, we find philosophies that are peculiar to each country. Japan and the U.S.S.R. emphasize precocity while Israel, Norway and Sweden view preschool education as a nurturing process and as a vehicle for the transmission of their cultural heritage. In England, priority is given to the disadvantaged as a sort of social reform. Indian educators believe that education should be available to the masses and not just to the elite. China and Mexico view education as a means of contributing to the growth of their nations. American programs aim at getting the child to understand himself and his environment. In Alberta, Canada, an attempt is made to strengthen the child's sense of dignity and self-worth.

A Ministry of Education or equivalent body is the controlling force in Japan, the U.S.S.R., Israel, China, Mexico, and England. Programs are under the auspices of the Social Welfare Department in India; the Community Services Administration of the Office of Education in the U.S.A.; the Ministry of Health and Social Affairs in Sweden; the Ministry of Consumer and Administration in Norway; and the Early Childhood Services Branch in Alberta, Canada.

All these countries have trained directors, teachers, aides, and support staff except China where programs are run mainly by housewives and young girls who undergo short, crash courses. In India, personnel attend courses varying from two months to twelve months in length, while the rest of the countries require their teachers to have two to four years of college training.

Preschool attendance is not compulsory in most of these countries. The types of programs in terms of location, size, objectives, etc. vary greatly. However, the majority consist of either in-home or center care.

Finances are provided either by the central governments, state governments, local bodies, or tuition charges. The breakdown by country is as follows in Table 12-I.

The curriculum varies from country to country and is a reflection of their different philosophies. Despite this variance, five main areas appear to be common in all the programs. They are physical, intellectual, language, and social development and the development of aesthetic appreciation, e.g. music, art, poetry.

Programs are held in specially constructed one-story buildings, although in the U.S.S.R. two- and three-story buildings are common. Rooms in primary schools are also used, as well as private

Table 12-I

Financing of Early Childhood Education

COUNTRY	CENTRAL GOVERNMENT	STATE (PROVINCIAL)	LOCAL	TUITION
U.S.S.R.	X			X
Israel			X	
India	X		X	
Japan	X		X	X
China	X			X
England	X		X	
U.S.A.	X	X	X	X
Mexico	X	X		X
Sweden	X		X	X
Norway	X		X	X
Alberta, Canada		X		

homes, churches, and community houses. Educational materials are in accordance with the different program objectives, while playground equipment is that which is common to most countries, although improvised materials are used in many cases.

The reader will be able to obtain an in-depth view of the different aspects of the programs in the countries discussed in the following sections.

PHILOSOPHY

U.S.S.R. Emphasizes precocity. A child could learn at an early age what he eventually will have to master.

Israel. Schools set up for the transmission of cultural heritage. Aims at development of child's personality and capacities and preparation for participation in life.

India. Preschool education should be available to the masses. Influence of Montessori and Froebel evident.

Japan. Education should begin as early as possible. Develops intellect, cultivates mind and body, and helps in social and moral development.

England. Originally a social reform movement. Presently, priority is given to disadvantaged children.

U.S.A. Combines the theories of Piaget, Dewey, and those of the British Infant School. Education deals with the child's social, emotional, cognitive, and motor development. Leads to a better understanding of self and environment.

Mexico. The development of the individual is a corollary to contributing to the society in which one lives.

Sweden. Based on theories of Gesell, Piaget, and Erikson. Emphasis is on child's personal and social development. An environment is provided that is socially and physically stimulating. Children can then discover their world.

Norway. Based on the theories of Rousseau, Pestallozi, Froebel, Decroly, Kilpatrick, Montessori, Isaacs, Piaget, and Gesell. Preschool education is basically a nurturing process.

Alberta, Canada. Central purpose is to strengthen the sense of dignity and self-worth within a child and his parents. Health, educational, social, emotional, and physical needs have to be met in cooperation with the home.

ADMINISTRATION

U.S.S.R. Directorate of Preschool Education in conjunction with joint commission of the Academy of Pedagogical Sciences of the Russian Republic and the Academy of Medical Sciences of the Soviet Union.

Israel. Special Department within the Ministry of Education and Culture.

India. Controlled by Director of Social Welfare within the Social Welfare Board.

Japan. Ministry of Education.

China. Run by local People's Councils, rural communes, urban factories, offices, industries, and residential areas. Regulations set by Central Ministry of Education.

England. Secretary of State for Education and Science. Nursery schools and classes, ages three to five, administered by Department of Education and Science. Day Nurseries, ages birth to five, administered by Department of Health and Social Security.

U.S.A. Community Services Administration of Office of Education.

Mexico. Office of General Director of Preschool Education, responsible to Minister of Education.

Sweden. Ministry of Health and Social Affairs. Actual supervision done by National Board of Health and Welfare.

Norway. Ministry of Consumers and Administration.

Alberta, Canada. Early Childhood Services Branch. Close cooperation with Department of Health and Social Development, Culture, Youth and Recreation, Advanced Education and Education.

PERSONNEL

U.S.S.R. Director (usually a woman), teachers, medical personnel, cook, domestic, and custodial help.

Israel. Teachers in Jewish schools are all women. Arab schools have 60 percent male teachers. Aides, rhythmics teacher, nurse, and other professionals available as needed.

India. Director, teachers, and aides.

Japan. Kindergarten—Director, teachers, nurses, clerks, physician, dentist, pharmacist. Day Nursery—Day nurses and part-time physician.

China. Housewives, young girls.

England. Head teacher, teachers, nursery nurses, sometimes a social worker.

U.S.A. Director, teachers and aides, medical personnel, cook, custodial.

Mexico. Director, teachers, other support staff.

Sweden. Director, teachers, nurses, kitchen staff, maintenance workers.

Norway. Director, support staff (could be parents).

Alberta, Canada. Director, teachers, aides, assistants, support staff.

TRAINING OF STAFF

U.S.S.R. College degree—training in child psychology, theories of learning, and other specialty areas.

Israel. Two to three years of training in teacher training colleges or seminaries. Kibbutz schools, three month seminars to full fledged teachers' courses.

India. Two to three month crash courses; eleven month certificate courses, one year courses.

Japan. Kindergarten – Bachelor's degree or junior college diploma. Day Nurseries–graduates of day nurse training institutes.

China. Most of the teachers are housewives (1970) or young girls who have undergone very short training courses.

England. Teachers are degreed. Nursery nurses–two years training.

U.S.A. Four or two year college training.

Mexico. Four year degree plus specialization, e.g. music, art, etc.

Sweden. Nursery schools–two year college. Preschools–four or two years of college. Day Care Mothers–ninety hour course in child care.

Norway. Teachers' course.

Alberta, Canada. Four year degree, with major in E.C.E.

EXTENT OF EARLY CHILDHOOD EDUCATION

U.S.S.R. Regular preschools, boarding schools, forest schools for unhealthy kids, schools for exceptional children.

Israel. 1976-1977: 5000 preschool classes: 165,000 children between ages three and six; Kibbutz schools.

India. Montessori schools, kindertartens, minimum-standard preschool, mobile creches for working mothers, laboratory preschools attached to universities. Enrollment, four million (1974).

Japan. 1977: Kindergarten enrollment – 65.1 percent of five-year-olds. Day Nursery enrollment – 25.4 percent of five-year-olds.

China. 1958: 90 percent literacy rate, 20 percent in 1949. Enrollment of forty-seven million.

England. 1976: 600 nursery schools; number of students full-time, 45,000; part-time, 100,000. Only 10 percent of children ages two to five in attendance. Programs also offered in preschool centers.

U.S.A. Programs offered through family child care, home play groups, parent/child/teacher programs, Child Care Aide Services,

Parent Cooperative Child Care Programs, and Head Start. These fall under three main types: In-home care (37%), Family day care (47%) and Center care (16%).

Mexico. 1978: 1000 preschools, 990 in Mexico City.

Sweden. Day nurseries, nursery schools, municipal family day nurseries, family day nurseries, recreation centers.

Norway. Programs run by private organizations, companies, hospitals, housewives organizations, church groups.

Alberta, Canada. Center programs, in-home programs, or a combination of the two. Parent programs are also offered and include workshops dealing with child-rearing and development practices.

FINANCING

U.S.S.R. Funded by state, tuition charges.

Israel. Funded by local bodies, no tuition charge.

India. Funded by state, contributions from the community and foreign programs such as CARE.

Japan. National Kindergartens—funded by government. Local Kindergartens—funded by the public. Private Kindergartens—funded by founders and through tuition charges. Day Nurseries—local contributions and tuition charges.

China. Funded by state, tuition.

England. Funded by government (65%) and local authorities (35%).

U.S.A. Funded by federal, state, and local authorities as well as by private groups, individuals, and parents, e.g. tuition, Community Chest.

Mexico. Federal and state funding, tuition. Physical plant provided by the government, equipment provided by parents.

Sweden. Funding shared among the state (35%), municipality (50%) and parents (15%). Parents pay tuition according to income level.

Norway. Subsidized by government; communities and parents contribute to operating costs; tuition is charged those who can afford it.

Alberta, Canada. Funded by provincial grants, which are contingent upon 540 hours of program offered on a half-day basis.

CURRICULUM

U.S.S.R. Physical and psychological development, language development, social skills, aesthetic appreciation, environmental orientation.

Israel. Predominantly content-centered and group-oriented.

India. Exercise in practical life, education of the senses, intellectual education, muscular education, language skills.

Japan. Health, social studies, nature, language, music and rhythm, drawing, handcrafts.

China. Music, productive labor, calisthenics, language skills, art, general knowledge.

England. Nursery schools—spontaneous play, physical activities, language skills, music, poetry, development of self-reliance, independence, and cooperation. Infant schools—language skills, early scientific and mathematical ideas, physical coordination, and the development of social relationships and aesthetic responses.

U.S.A. Music, reading, sand and water play, blockbuilding, games, and domestic skills.

Mexico. Health, hygiene, recreation, patriotism, arts, family, school, and social awareness.

Sweden. Social, emotional, physical, and intellectual development, self-help skills, fine and gross motor skills, respect for rules and prohibitions, ability to communicate effectively with others.

Norway. Emphasis on free-play periods, which encourages self-awareness, language and intellectual development, the acquisition of basic skills, and the development of a good self-concept.

Alberta, Canada. Language skills, basic skills, cognitive, emotional, affective, motor, perceptual, and social development, development of self-concept.

FACILITIES

U.S.S.R. Two-story buildings for nurseries, three-story buildings for some nurseries. Playground equipment, educational materials.

Israel. Specially constructed buildings near an elementary school. Two classes in one building sharing common amenities. Playground equipment, educational materials. Kibbutz—children's houses.

India. Buildings, under a tree, court yards, verandah of a school. Playground equipment, educational materials.

Japan. One-story buildings. Adequate facilities for education, health, sanitation, administrative, and playing areas.

China. Individual buildings, rooms in primary schools. Playground and educational materials.

England. One-story buildings. Space for outdoor play and for gardens, sheltered play areas, room for parents, play, and educational materials.

U.S.A. One-story buildings. Classes allow freedom of movement, have different learning centers and materials.

Mexico. Single-story buildings, adequate facilities for education, health, sanitation, administration, and playing areas.

Sweden. One-story buildings, play equipment, learning materials.

Norway. Private homes, school buildings, churches, community houses, specially built schools. Educational and playground materials.

Alberta, Canada. Single-story buildings, flexible room arrangements, learning and activity centers, playground equipment, learning materials as required by program objectives.

Early childhood educators, despite their national and philosophical differences, have the interests of the preschool child at heart. They are very much interested in his social, emotional, cognitive, and motor development. They want their children to have every opportunity for developing into well-rounded individuals, individuals who will bring about an improvement in their communities, who will make a lasting contribution to their countries, and above all, make the world a better place in which to live. By working together, educators can and will see this dream fulfilled.

We may not have much control over political situations, other circumstances, or even our own destinies, yet, we have the glorious opportunity of working with young children, of guiding them, of developing their mental, physical, and spiritual powers. It is this task that early childhood educators have been called to fulfill, and it is sincerely hoped that this volume has in some way rekindled that commitment.

INDEX